The Guide to Getting In

The Guide to Getting In

Winning the College Admissions Game Without Losing Your Mind

A Guide from Harvard Student Agencies

Danielle Charbonneau   Editor
Arianne Cohen   Associate Editor

Writers

Olivia L. Cowley

Kathy H. Lee

Thomas L. Miller

Michael E. Yank

St. Martin's Griffin
New York

www.stmartins.com

Library of Congress Cataloging-in-Publication Data

The guide to getting in : winning the college admissions game without losing your mind / Danielle Charbonneau, editor ; Arianne Cohen, associate editor ; writers, Olivia L. Cowley ... [et al.].—1st ed.
    p.cm.
    "A guide from Harvard Student Agencies."
    ISBN 0-312-30044-1
    1. Universities and colleges—United States—Admission—Handbooks, manuals, etc. I. Charbonneau, Danielle. II. Cohen, Arianne. III. Cowley, Olivia L. IV. Harvard Student Agencies.

    LB2351.2.G83 2002
    378.1'61'0973--dc21   2002024863

10 9 8 7 6 5 4 3

Contents

Acknowledgments

Founded in 1957, Harvard Student Agencies, Inc. (HSA) exists to provide Harvard students with a practical business experience while providing useful services for the Harvard community and helping to defray the cost of college tuition. HSA is the world's largest student-run corporation, and encompasses ten divisions, including the Harvard Bartending Course, Unofficial Publications, the Harvard Shop, and Let's Go Publishing, which produces the series of bestselling budget travel guides.

While we have been publishing books at our office in Cambridge for years, *The Guide to Getting In* has been an entirely new type of project for us, and it is only through the tireless work of many devoted individuals that it is in your hands today. In addition to an incredibly talented editorial team, I would like to thank a few of the many people who worked diligently behind the scenes to bring you this book: Melissa Rudolph, a longtime Let's Go veteran, for her innovative design and typesetting work; Lani Arceo, Sarah Tavel, Susan Mathai, Abhishek Gupta, and Sarah Rotman, for their continual advice and support; Esti Iturralde, HSA alumna and our editor at St. Martin's Press; Cindy Rodriguez, former HSA president; Robert Rombauer, HSA General Manager; and Anne Chisholm, HSA Assistant General Manager.

We hope you have as much fun reading this book as we did writing it. Good luck as you begin to navigate the college admissions process.

—Bradley J. Olson,
President, Harvard Student Agencies, Inc.

A Note to Our Readers...

We really do understand.

Everyone you talk to lately wants to know where you're applying to school, what your essays are about, and what you want to study when you get to wherever it is you're going. We know how irritating it gets to hear about every uncle's college football days and your hairdresser's daughter at, what was the name of that college again? Oh, yes, I've heard of that, um, that's a good school! Just remember, they are trying to help. Someday you'll be at parties telling high school–aged folk about your college mischief, too, and your mom will be telling all the ladies at her salon about where her daughter goes to school. It's just the way of the world these days.

So with all the questions and advice flying at you, this is likely a pretty stressful time. We know it is. It wasn't all that long ago that we were right there ourselves, you know! But we made it, and in retrospect, it's kind of cool. Pretty soon, you'll be miles from home and you probably still aren't sure just where. It's like you're on the edge of dropping into the rest of your life and don't know yet where that will land you. All that unknown out there, and it's up to you to decide where you go. When was the last time you got to make such a big leap at your own choosing? Keeping that in mind, this all might strike you as exciting or nerve-racking, or both. In any case, you're probably in good shape if you've sat down to read our book, and we hope it does you some good.

With our collective heads together, we've come up with a guide for the often confusing, always stressful process of admissions. We've tried to answer the very questions that we asked along the way with the things that we found worked best. Our advice certainly isn't final, and we don't pretend to be the Bible of College Admissions, but we do know some things from playing the game ourselves that your counselors can't tell you, and that the admissions people think you'll figure out yourself. In short, we know how to get into college, we just did it, and now we want to help you get here, too.

Our message is really simple: relax. This whole admissions game is just that: a game. Once you know the rules of the game, you can just get out there and play, and practice will only make you better at it. If you think of every uncle and hairdresser who has ever tried to ask you about college, you'll realize you're getting better at answering the questions they ask every time. When someone first asked you what you were looking for in a school, you probably didn't have much to answer. But the more times you get asked that question (and have to answer it while pretending you haven't been asked it three times that day), the smoother and more polished your answers become to exactly the kinds of questions that colleges need you to be able to answer. In most cases, your elders kind of know this, and they wouldn't be asking except they want you to start thinking of answers, because they think you can make it. So it's a great compliment, really. That, or they just have very little else to talk about. But either way, you'll get some practice and you'll come off as such a well-spoken kid.

So just think—everyone who asks you about your plans for the next few months is a practice ball for you to swing at. By the time an admissions officer wants to know what you think of their school, you'll have a perfect swing.

It just makes you wanna smooch Uncle Harry and your hairdresser.

—Danielle Charbonneau, Editor

CHAPTER ONE

High School

An Era of Hall Passes, P.E., and Cafeteria Romance

We'd be lying if we said we're sad to be out of high school. Heck, the sheer thrill of leaving a class to go pee without asking permission is still exhilarating, and the last time any of us were awake at 7 A.M., it was because we hadn't gone to bed yet. But high school, despite its plethora of shortcomings, is still worth the four-year commitment. It's not only the price of the ticket to college, but it's a piece of yourself that you will always remember. But how will you remember it? As the time in your life most complicated by sleep deprivation? As a great period of learning? Or as a little of both?

The truth is high school is hard! Applying to college is almost fun compared to your last AP chem test, or explaining for the billionth time why you were late to homeroom. Filling out application forms is a great way to procrastinate doing yet another outline for history class ("suck it Teapot Dome Scandal!") But it's all the more fun if it's your chance to brag about all the great things you did despite an overwhelming urge to sleep past 6:30 A.M.

The best advice we can possibly give you about getting through the high school years—and this goes for everyone from the jock-strapped to the pocket-protected—is to *passionately follow your interests*. The secret to success is to participate in the things that you really do love, and participate with great enthusiasm. *Passion* is the key. We'll talk more about that later.

Classes: Easy As or Impressive Honors?

We've all done it: fantasized about a schedule filled with beginner's photo and yoga, planned a scheme to convince administration that you should be in English as a second language, even though you were born in Duluth. But all those easy As won't impress anyone, especially those super-savvy people at the admissions office. "But," you protest, "I can't take eight AP classes a day *and* get great grades!" That's OK, too. The secret is to do what you can as much and as well as possible, and we can show you how.

It's simple, really. Take the most challenging courses you can while keeping your grade point average high, your activities and interests afloat, oh, and staying sane. It might seem weird to have two personalities, but now one can sleep while the other writes your English paper. If this seems obvious, good for you and your other personality. The rest of us might require some more explanation.

If taking an honors-level course would stress you out massively, ruin your GPA, or make you hate life altogether, don't do it. Do what's best for you according to your academic level. But if taking honors courses is challenging but feasible, do it! Colleges will appreciate your efforts in honors courses where you maintain acceptable grades (an absolute B minimum, preferably B+ or above.)

Feasibility is not enough; interest helps a lot, too. That AP Physics class will look impressive on your record, but if you've had just about enough of that know-it-all Newton, and you'd be happier in Advanced Biology because you really like animals (even the ones you have to cut up), your greater interest will translate to better grades.

Your level of interest, unfortunately, cannot be the only factor in your choice of classes. Remember while choosing all of those basket-weaving courses that you have "genuine" interest in that most colleges have minimum requirements that you must meet. (We'll go over these later.) Moreover, in many cases, more challenging courses are weighted heavier than others, so those baskets might hurt more than help your class rank. If going to a great college *is* what interests you, then you'll need to take the toughest stuff you can tackle.

Handle as much as you can, show that you are willing to face challenges, but don't pretend you can cut it if you can't. You should look at high school as a good way to gauge what kind of college you should go to later. If you can't handle AP chem now, you won't handle a competetive chemical engineering program at the nation's toughest colleges. Admissions officers know this, and although in most cases they will respect you for undertaking academic challenges, failing at those challenges doesn't help you very much. Also, failure is kind of depressing, which might be tough to handle with only that one personality.

Ultimately, admissions officers will compare your course-load to the courses *offered* at your school. Each officer has a region that he or she covers, and is intimately familiar with the course options and grading policies at individual high schools. This means that if your high school only offers one advanced place-ment course and you're in it, you're doing fine. However, if your high school offers thirty honors courses, and the admissions office sees that you've attempted only a few, then your essay tout-ing your strong desire to learn might take on the figurative smell of garbage, and end up in the same place.

Colleges realize that your extracurricular activities may be time consuming, and they do believe in sleep. There's no need to be an insomniac or hook an IV of coffee to your arm—feel free to maintain normal resting hours, a lunch period, and a social life, because if you don't, you'll be a burnt-out emotional wrecking ball long before you even arrive on campus. Most college applica-tions ask how many hours you spend on various activities each week, giving admissions officers a clear idea of how you spend your time.

So with your ideal extracurricular schedule in mind, pick a courseload that's best for your lifestyle while allowing you an aca-demic challenge. Picking activities and classes that really do interest you will make it easier to achieve lots of accolades without feeling too stressed out. As hard as it might seem to balance the three hardest science classes at your high school while founding a student ecology group and holding an after-school job at the local laboratories, it's a heck of a lot easier if you like science.

Whatever your academic choices, make sure that you've taken the required courses for the colleges you are applying to. No matter how wonderful you are, if you ignore a college's requirements, they'll ignore you. For most top-choice schools of higher education, the requirements resemble the chart below. It's preferable to take the recommended rather than just the required:

Subject	Required	Recommended
English	4 yrs.	4 yrs.
Mathematics	2 yrs.	4 yrs.
Science	2 yrs. + 1 yr. lab	4 yrs.
History / Social Sciences	2+1	4 yrs.
Foreign Language	2 yrs. of same	4 yrs. of same

Academic Attitude

It is pivotal to start taking academics seriously in ninth grade—you really don't want to start off slowly enjoying the scenery, potentially ruining your class rank for senior year. Many high schools, particularly larger ones, employ some form of academic tracking system where high-honors, honors, regular, and, well, sub-regular students take their own classes: a complete aca-

More than 50 percent of adults surveyed said that children should not be paid money for getting good grades in school.

Source:
www.uselessknowledge.com

demic segregation system. A freshman year spent watching trees grow could leave you in a track lower than where you deserve to be. It's much easier to start in a higher track and stay there than it is to play academic catch-up for three years (though you will have a superior knowledge of tree growth).

A poor academic reputation can be very harmful—after freshman year, teachers often have access to the academic transcripts of their incoming students, and even though students are supposedly graded solely on the work done in each class, you don't want to be labeled a chronic C student. In all schools, teachers tend to gossip (though they may deny it) in faculty rooms about students, particularly about the best, worst, and most poorly behaved students. If you can develop a reputation as a good student or as an asset to the classroom, half your work will already be done for you, as teachers will expect you to be good before you even enter their class. This is a great way to avoid having to prove yourself worthy of good grades with each individual course.

But let's say you have a poor reputation, or you just need to improve it a little, are you doomed? Heck no. Meet with teachers outside of class to show your interest and personality. Good teachers will always respond well to student interest, and your effort will pay off in both a better appreciation of the material and improved grades, both because of your increased understanding of the material and the teacher's increased understanding of you. A junior from the University of Texas told us that until the ninth grade she had been pegged as a clone of her two older sisters, both of whom were real problem children who generally made teachers run in fear. "So I just told them one day. I like class more than my sisters did. . . . I'm not going to be like them so don't treat me like I'm a problem before I even open my mouth!" That UT junior found that her teacher always heard her out after that, and they actually became close friends. So don't be afraid to stand up for yourself if you're getting a bad rap!

Many students will exhibit temporarily low grades at some point in their high school careers, perhaps due to freshman-year academic adjustment or personal crises. Such discrepancies will not be penalized much at all in the admissions office if explained somewhere else in the application—either in a letter of recommendation, your essay, or by the college guidance counselor. One of the writers of this book got a few Cs in high school. Although we can't tell you which one, we can tell you that with a little explaining, she still got into Harvard! So that tiny little C, though it hurts you so, isn't reason enough to burn all of your bulk-rate college mail in the front yard.

Still, it is better to avoid grade slips whenever possible. Keep in mind that a grade slip, by definition, cannot be permanent—you do need to recover at some point. Slips are acceptable, but permanently low grades mean you have not, and maybe will never, recover from the academic slump you've hit, and that makes colleges worry. You will not be able to sell your overachieving, straight-A freshman self to the admissions office after a two-year slump—that's like trying to sell a broken television. Sure, it worked once, and it might work great once it's fixed, but that doesn't make anyone too excited to buy it when there are so many out there that do work. Who you used to be isn't as important to them as who you are, so hop to and get those grades in order.

Finding a Purpose

Your feelings toward high school academics are a strong indicator of what kind of college you'll eventually seek out. If the terms "calculus," "differential," and "titration" make you want to cry and drop out of school, your talents may lie in more artistic or literary areas that can be further developed in the appropriate class setting—but tech school probably isn't for you. On the other hand, if essay questions often cause a flaming ball of anxiety in your stomach, you might want to shy away from communications or journalism schools. So it's important to take a moment and ask yourself basic questions, such as, "What am I interested in?" "How am I using my high school years?" "Am I taking advantage of the opportunities available to me?" "Why do I study?" and "Do I need a haircut?"

The answers to such life-goal questions will be very apparent on your college applications. Whether you like it or not, college admissions officers are extremely savvy at reading between the lines (i.e. identifying B.S.), and when presented with your academic transcript, personal essay, letters of recommendation, and a profile of your high school, it will be crystal clear how you spent the last three-and-a-half years. If the answers to the above questions are not much more than, "How the hell should I know?" you'll want to find some direction now while you still can. For example, if you're not sure what you're doing in high school or what you're really interested in, you may want to sit down and talk to a friend or teacher about what classes would better interest you, and how you could better use the opportunities available to you while becoming more involved in high school life. If you study only for your parents, you'll want to think long and hard before wasting their money at the college of their dreams, and may want to schedule a meeting with your college guidance counselor, no matter how useless he or she is. And if you need a haircut, get a haircut.

Ultimately, admissions officers will want to know one thing: how you'll *contribute* to their college. Contribution isn't all test grades—it's involvement with the entire academic community,

pause

1. A hesitation by an admissions officer looking over your file.

2. An admissions concern raised by something in your application.

3. Something to avoid at all costs.

4. Very, very bad.

from classroom discussions to extracurriculars, from the way you accept criticism to the way you interact with teachers and other students. If you're a jerk, they'll hear about it; if you're an asset to discussion, they'll hear about that, too. Whether you're a genuine student or a genuine grade grubber will show in your letters of recommendation. Admissions officers want to hear that you love to learn, so speak up!

A Word on Shyness

Many students struggle with shyness, a trait that will only become more problematic if not overcome early on. Shyness inherently inhibits participation in intellectual discussion, so not only will your high school teachers not necessarily know how wonderful you are, your admissions officers will have to *pause* to ask themselves how much you will contribute to their university classes. Admissions officer pauses are always bad, so if you are generally quiet, it's important to make a genuine effort to speak up in class and in life, too. Talking is fun—it's how you learn about gossip pivotal to your social life. So join the debate club, take a public speaking class, act in a play production, run for office, anything that will get you talking. In the long run, shyness will only thwart your path to success. If there's something you want to say in class, say it. Unless it has no relevance—because you'll have to sit there and think of a way to relate the lack of pop-tarts at today's lunch to the love between Dido and Aeneas, which is *really* hard to do. (Trust us.)

Extracurriculars

Extracurricular activities are your chance to have fun, make friends, and enjoy non-academic interests in an organized fashion; so get out there and have a good time! Heck, it beats working. How you spend your free time is your opportunity to show colleges where your priorities lie and what you're passionate about. If you tout your interest in activism, for example, you'd better be out there cleaning streets and caring for sick baby dolphins rather than just admonishing people who don't. If you're hoping to show them you love to write, telling them might be nice, but telling them that you edited a literary magazine or wrote editorials for the school newspaper hits it home just a hair harder. High school is your big opportunity to do what you love; so get crazy and get into it! As we've said, find something you can love and commit to it.

You can use your freshman year to explore as many options as you want, and then streamline them over time.

Streamlining is key. Being a member of every club in school, sleeping three hours a night, and taking classes on your lunch hour is not only painful, but it doesn't show commitment to anything other than masochism. By senior year, you should only be participating in the activities that you truly love, and on which you yourself have had an impact. Did you do anything for the Spanish club this year other than sign the attendance sheet? Maybe it's not the right club for you then. Spend whole weekends organizing fund-raisers for the band? Admissions officers will admire your dedication, and hey, you must really like band.

Another thing to keep in mind is that admissions officers appreciate extracurricular challenges the way they appreciate academic challenges. Any admissions officer will know that as president of the Backgammon club, your duties were probably not over- whelmingly challenging. How- ever, if you created a new comm- unity service club and now man- age its finances, the admissions officer will be impressed. In other words, your time is better spent on a few important activities that you are really devoted to than on a dozen that you are not.

If a college feels that your pri- orities are worthwhile enough, your extracurriculars can actually compensate for other parts of your application that might not be so strong. Colleges reward excel- lence, including musical or ath- letic achievement, and realize that excellence in one field might mean less focus on grades, as in the case of world-class athletes who miss school for international tournaments. This is because, in

U.S. Presidents who never went to col- lege: Grover Cleve- land, Abraham Lincoln, and Harry S. Truman.

U.S. Presidents who went to Harvard: John Adams, John Quincy Adams, Rutherford B. Hayes, Theodore Roosevelt, Franklin Delano Roosevelt, John F. Kennedy, and George W. Bush.

balance

1. Belonging to every club, from the school literary journal to the Pi club, so that instead of excelling in one arena, you're mediocre in many.

2. Belonging to every club, but not taking on leadership roles of any kind in any club.

3. Spread too thin, like half a teaspoon of peanut butter on an entire bagel.

recent years, colleges have shifted from rewarding "balance" to rewarding "excellence."

They used to say that "well-rounded kids" did the best in the college admissions game, which was misconstrued over time to mean "balanced" kids. Admissions officers know that "balanced" can just mean a lack of focus. So that crowded box of activities can be a flag against you rather than for you. However, if you are well-rounded and *also excellent* at everything—winning the Intel competition on the same day your novel goes to press—you clearly will have no problem getting into college. Very few are outstanding at everything, but being mediocre at everything isn't more impressive to college admissions officers than being excellent at the things that interest you most.

Admissions wants to see that you know how to convert effort into achievement. This is your time to put effort into something you love. That effort will be rewarded whether it's toward a school-oriented activity (e.g., editor of the school newspaper, president of the math club, captain of the swim team) or toward something completely outside of school (e.g., horse show champion, world-class ice fisher). As long as your venture is worthwhile to you and your life, your admissions officer will like it.

An important thing to remember about all of this is that at some point you will have to talk about your activities, whether in a short essay or in the interview (shriek!). This is a whole lot easier if you really care about what you've been doing. Admissions officers will know if you're feigning enthusiasm for the beekeeper's society, and they won't like it.

Excellence will usually be rewarded over widespread balance. However, it is recommended that

excellence

1. Excelling in one arena.

2. A quality, worthwhile use of time.

3. An obvious show of long-term determination and hard work, paying off in a brilliant sweep of achievement.

4. Your ticket to college acceptance.

you try to show interest in more than one area. Your two main activities might be, say, school and running, but a membership in a youth group or book club is always a nice touch to show diversity in your life and knowledge in other areas. You can belong to as many organizations as you like, as long as you either really love them or excel in them—preferably both. The admissions game will reward hard work and excellence, both of which will be a likely result when you do something you love.

Summers: Go Join the Circus

You only have three of them, so have fun!

The same guidelines that apply to extracurricular activities apply to your summertime activities, except that the summertime allows more flexibility because you are not constrained by a six-hour school day. How you spend your summers speaks volumes about your priorities. It speaks enough, in fact, that if you haven't indicated how you spent your Junes, Julys, and Augusts on your application, your interviewer will definitely ask. A junior at Boston University told us that her Harvard interviewer wanted to know what she did while vacationing with her family in Europe one summer. "I spent a lot of time on the beach," she answered, "I didn't really want to walk around much." She thought this was an amusing joke to tell, but the interviewer certainly didn't laugh. This college candidate wasted her rare opportunity of a trip to Europe, and her interviewer took this as a clear sign that she might waste her opportunity at Harvard. You should think of every summer as an opportunity to show those admissions people that you don't fool around with your free time.

So get out there and do something with all that time. Take a leap, do something crazy, and have fun, but please tighten your harness before you jump, or you'll never make it to college.

Summer internships are a great option, allowing you to decide whether you're really interested in what you think you're interested in (seemingly great jobs aren't always all they're chalked up to be). You can also make contacts for possible letters of recommendation, which offer a valuable insight into your work ethic. Internships in off-beat places, such as whitewater rafting companies or design houses can be amazingly fun. Internships are often flexible and part-time, such as three days a week or half-days, leaving you plenty of time to pursue other important activities, such as hanging out with your friends.

We encourage you, however, to beware of internships that will leave you filing papers in the boiling hot basement of the office of your dreams for an entire summer. Sweating onto files for three months just isn't a fun or worthwhile experience, and your boss might be angered by the drip marks on her invoices. To prevent this, speak honestly to employers as to exactly what your duties will include long before you agree to an internship, and be sure you know what you're in for with internships that include "secretarial work" and "general assistant duties," unless, of course, you're really passionate about office-style organization.

Many students spend their summers furthering their talents in their areas of expertise, spending their time training for athletics,

**secretarial work/
general assistant
duties**

1. Fourteen daily
hours of photocopy-
ing, in the only non-
air-conditioned sec-
tion of the building.

2. Copier will jam
frequently, at which
point you'll kick it
hard, and then again
harder, building leg
muscles.

3. Hellish summer
job, except for those
who are delighted by
paperwork. (Such
people do exist, and
they get excited by
post-it flags and
three hole punches—
we kid you not.)

participating in music programs,
and attending summer academic
programs. Such ventures will definitely be rewarded by your
admissions officer, because they
exhibit commitment (even over
the summer, wow!) and determination toward a goal. These programs also indicate where a
student's true interests lie, giving
your top-choice school an idea of
what activities you might participate in at their college, and how
you might contribute to their academic environment.

Workin' It

Get a job . . . and have you cut your
hair yet! Summertime or term-
time, regardless of whether or
not you need the money, admissions officers like to see that you
have held a job. Working shows
both a work ethic and time management ability, two skills necessary for success in college.

Taking on a job allows you to show your willingness to work, while further expanding your experience and talents. Jobs are also a great chance to learn skills that will pop up later in life. For example, if you work as a bus-person in an upscale restaurant and constantly have to cooperate with a difficult manager, you'll know better how to react when your kleptomaniac freshman-year roommate accuses you of stealing the stapler that was actually yours in the first place. Admissions officers know that such scenarios might come up, and they just want you to be prepared.

Get a job even if you don't need the money. Many admissions officers develop an automatic bias against affluent students who have seemingly had their lives handed to them on a silver platter. (After comparing the students of the finest preparatory schools to students who have overcome adversity in lousy inner-city schools, it's understandable that such a bias might develop, particularly if the officer had to work for his or her own education.) Taking on a job allows you to combat this bias, while developing skills you would never have otherwise learned, such as the fine art of ice cream scooping, toilet plunging, or water-cooler gossiping.

Although working experience is unanimously considered an asset, if your job is compromising your studies or extracurricular life, ditch it. Academics come first, always. Admissions officers will understand jobless applicants who devote extraordinary amounts of time to other commitments, such as in the case of amazing athletes or budding scientists. Still, if there's any way for you to maintain employment without sacrificing your transcript, do it. Many jobs will allow you to work only one shift a week,

---

do-nothing jobs

1. Employment that requires little more than your occasional bodily presence.

2. Example: Late-night library clerk.

3. Example: Athletic facility front desk person.

4. Example: Security guard at a locale that doesn't actually warrant security.

---

maybe four hours on a Saturday, and this good-faith effort will be rewarded in admissions offices. We also highly recommend *do-nothing jobs.*

Many do-nothing jobs are a wonderful opportunity to study and will help you raise your grades, because really, what else is there to do while sitting guard at the local Natural History museum?

Read

The most useful extracurricular activity we can recommend is reading. SAT I verbal scores have been shown to improve with higher frequency of recreational reading, and reading books is a great stimulus for your brain. Though higher-quality works of writing such as *The New Yorker* and Tolstoy will probably be more advantageous to your education, if you like *MAD Magazine* or Jackie Collins's books or even comic strips, read 'em. Recreational reading should be just that—enjoyable recreation, not a hell that you avoid. Tuck a book into your backpack for the bus, free periods, or your downtime at summer circus camp. Really, reading anywhere, anytime will directly pay off, such as when your interviewer asks you what your favorite book is, you answer, and he happens to be an expert on that author. Having actually read the book will be pivotal in this situation. That previously mentioned junior from BU ran into more trouble during her Harvard interview when she told her interviewer that she'd "been really into Kerouac for the last few years," but then could only remember that he wrote *On the Road*. It ended up looking like she either took a few years to complete one book or she was trying to pull one over on

In 2001, nearly 60 percent of U.S. high schools participated in the AP Program. In that same year, more than 840,000 students took 1.4 million AP Exams.

Source: AP Program

her interviewer. I think we all know what the interviewer knew then: she hadn't done much reading and was trying to make herself look better.

Don't Sell Yourself Short

Now that you've picked the perfect extracurriculars to complement your talents and schedule, make sure to put *all* of your major high school activities on your application. (We're assuming this is implied, but you never know.) Many students will spend hours upon hours each week babysitting for siblings and never put it on their application. If you read four books a week, put that down. If you mow the lawns for your entire apartment development, put that down, too. At the very least, listing these extras accounts for your seemingly free time. At best, they display a work ethic and some different non-academic interests. Otherwise, it is assumed that you spend all free hours "hanging out," and admissions is not a big fan of "hanging out."

We recommend that starting freshman year, you keep a list somewhere of all the activities that you've been involved in, so that by the time senior year rolls around, you remember what you've been up to for the past three years and can tell admissions officers how wonderful you really are. The list can be as simple as the major activities you participated in, as detailed as all the books you read, or all the hours you volunteered. The truth is, if you can't remember what you did fall of sophomore year, the admissions officer reading your application goes to the default

COLLEGE COUNSELORS **23**

"hanging out," which is a real shame if you were up at eight every weekend to help the elderly rake leaves.

College Counselors

Your college counselor will be either your biggest asset in your college search or a useless piece of administrative flack. Usually, college counselors have seen hundreds upon hundreds of students go through the admissions process and can help guide you. Sometimes they have seen hundreds upon hundreds of students go through the admissions process but still find the process foreign and confusing. We are unsure what these type of counselors are paid to do, but beware of them. Even the editors of this book had problems with their high school guidance counselors. One guidance counselor went so far as to laugh at the mention of Harvard, saying it was "just a little harder" than anything this student could get into. Without help from her, this student ended up getting in early. After that, she was the one laughing for the next six months. So don't think just because at the start of senior year they still call you by your older sister's name (and you're a boy) that you're doomed in the college admissions game—you can do it alone if need be. But do try to use them to your advantage if you can. Set up a meeting early in your high school career (even during freshman year, gasp!) just to get acquainted. Introduce yourself, and ask for advice on what opportunities you may have looked over in your high school, as well as what activities and classes he or she recommends.

Even if your counselor is completely useless, he or she will be contacting the schools of your dreams, so be nice. All college counselors will eventually pen an evaluation of you, including your character, and this evaluation can be pivotal in the eyes of an admissions officer, swinging borderline cases one way or the other. The average or below-average counselor doesn't get to know too many students personally, so taking the initiative to develop a professional relationship can pay off immensely—just be nice and be yourself (unless you're inherently evil, in which case you would want to pretend to be someone else).

Independent Counselors

As college admissions becomes increasingly competitive, many students search out independent college counselors to aid them with their college searches. To meet this demand, there are hundreds of private college counselors who, for usually exorbitant fees, promise to match you up with and help you gain acceptance to the college of your dreams. Many of these professionals are quite knowledgeable in their field, and many are not.

The hiring of such consultants is generally unnecessary. If you happen to fall under one of the following four categories, however, you might consider a private counselor (although it still isn't, by any stretch, necessary.)

You may want to consider a private counselor if...
1. Your high school is extremely large, and your college counselor will not have time to appropriately guide you through the college process.

You may want to consider a private counselor if...
2. Your high-school college counselor is either non-existent, or rather useless. (In such cases, other teachers may gain reputations for giving wonderful college advice, but they will probably not have the time to give you the attention you deserve.)
3. You have a special talent that can only be further developed at certain schools, and would benefit from the counsel of a specialist in this area.
4. You have special educational needs, and would profit from the guidance of an expert in special needs.

If you do fall under one of these categories and seek out an independent college counselor, it's best to meet early in your high-school career so that they know and understand you. They will also like you more because you will have forked over more money for a longer period of time.

Use the introductory meeting to decide whether or not a counselor is qualified to help you. What does he or she envision for your college search? At what type of school does he or she see you? What type of experience does this person have? Can you talk to former clients? Is this counselor an expert in the special considerations of your college search? Does he or she need a haircut? If you don't feel fully confident in an independent counselor in the first meeting, keep looking. Just because he or she is very nice doesn't mean they deserve to be your college counselor.

Aside from these categories, there is little reason for hiring an independent college counselor. Much of the initial college

The Harvard Class of 2005:

—faced the worst odds of admittance in Harvard's history at 10.7 percent.

—has more women (at 49 percent) than any other in the college's long history.

Source: The Harvard Gazette

search process can take place in your own library, with your looking up various schools in books and on the Internet. You can usually handle the bulk of the college process on your own and use a college counselor for general guidance.

Listen to Your Elders

Another often-untapped college resource is the advice of students above you at your school. As an underclassman, you have the opportunity to watch older students experience the college search. Talk to them, both during and after, and they'll openly tell you about the pitfalls and loopholes of the college process. (If they're crying, wait a few days.) Though high school freshmen and sophomores usually try to avoid the college process for as long as is physically possible, watching students from similar backgrounds advance through the maze of college admissions is an invaluable tool.

For example, if one of your school's college counselors is useless, but one of the history teachers is a former admissions officer and knows everything there is to know about college admissions, an older student will know. If certain teachers write weak letters of recommendation, the students will know that, too. If the football players at a certain school are really cute, they'll know. If you need a haircut, they'll tell you! So ask.

How It All Adds Up

Admissions officers will eventually be considering your high-school career under three main categories: academics, extracurriculars, and personal characteristics. Any one of these categories

Evidence compiled by the Washington Homeschool Research Project suggests that home-schooled students perform as well or better than other students on standardized tests.

"High School is much harder than college."

—Senior, Harvard University (with Phi Beta Kappa standing)

"College is much harder than high school."

—Senior, Harvard University (not Phi Beta Kappa standing)

has the power to either compensate for another not-so-strong category, or to thwart your chances altogether.

For example, a student whose academic record is below average for the school to which she's applying will benefit greatly from a resume deep with extracurricular excellence and positions of leadership, as well as glowing letters of recommendation citing her friendly demeanor and wonderful work ethic. This student has a great chance of acceptance, despite her less-than-perfect academic record.

On the flipside, a seemingly great student with top grades and a slew of extracurriculars might be irreparably hurt by recommendations that seem hesitant about his social skills and hint that his motivation is grades only, with little actual interest in the class material.

There are always cases of quote endquote *"perfect students"* who surprise high school communities into lots of "I can't believe so-and-so wasn't accepted, and so-and-so was!" gossip.

The problem with the perfect student is that nothing about him or her stands out to an admissions committee, especially at a top-notch college. Such a student doesn't really seem to excel in anything, and doesn't seem, from the point of view of an admissions committee, to be particularly interested in or passionate about anything. Keep in mind that there are thousands of other "perfect" students applying to the top schools in the country, and only those who show some measure of being outstanding in some area will actually get in. Simply not messing up yet isn't really good enough when it comes to college.

perfect student

1. A student with an impressive academic record, a full extracurricular schedule, and pleasant letters of recommendation.

2. Considered a shoe-in at all of the top colleges.

3. Not actually a shoe-in at any of the top colleges.

For these reasons, packaging yourself as just another "perfect student" is not advisable. Make them, no, make everyone remember your love and dedication to something, even if its something that not everyone knows or loves. Be different; it's like putting a shiny blue star on your application for them to find and know you by. If that shiny blue star is something that makes them smile when they think about it, you're in. If there are no blue stars to remember, all the perfect grades and test scores and recommendations in all the world couldn't save your application from being thrown into a sea of identical perfect applications. How would they find it again? Answer: they won't. Those shiny blue stars are what bring home the heavy envelopes.

CHAPTER TWO

Tiny Bubbles

The World of Standardized Testing

If you've never taken a standardized test before, imagine this scene: you're in a poorly ventilated classroom with uncomfortable seats, surrounded by a bunch of strangers whose furious calculator button-pressing tears into your brain like so many knives—knives like the ones you wish you could plunge into the heart of the insidious demon at ETS who wrote the question for which you are currently writing out endless pages of long division. You struggle to grab at your last #2 pencil ("Lucky"), whose graphite point is now duller than your AP Physics teacher, as the eighty-year-old woman proctoring the exam calls out the dreaded death knell: "Time!" You have answered only a handful of the questions with certainty, and guessed on the rest of them. For many people, standardized tests are slightly worse than this. For you, however, lucky reader, taking standardized tests will be much less painful: you've got us on your side! In this section, we will explain how these all-too-dreaded examinations work, which will allow you to enter them with confidence. Don't forget that despite all the tiny fill-in bubbles, they are, after all, only tests, just like the ones you've been taking since you were in elementary school.

What Are Standardized Tests?

Standardized tests are exactly what they sound like—tests customized by a guy named Stan Dard—but seriously—they're just tests administered to students in a standard, particular way, on the same day, and everybody gets the same questions. That means that there's a kid taking the SATs across the country the same day you are, and he might be stuck on the very question that's causing your head to throb . . . creepy!

Your scores on standardized tests work with your grades to give colleges a fuller picture of what you know. Among other things, the exams will give you a chance to prove that you really *are* good at geometry (and that Mr. Troy only gave you that C+ because he hated you), but can also expose any grade inflation that you might have enjoyed at your cushy high school, so be careful!

The following describes the tests you are likely to come across.

The SAT: The Biggie

Consisting of both verbal and mathematical sections, the Scholastic Aptitude[1] Test is taken by over two million students every year. But don't be intimated by this statistic: more than half of

---

1.While the "A" in SAT originally stood for "Aptitude," it was later officially changed to "Assessment," and many others since have also believed it to stand for "Achievement." However, the College Board (which produces and administers the SAT) has since declared that "SAT is not an initialism." Apparently the three-letter name has transcended acronymity to become something more divine. In other words, while your scores may mean something, the name of the test does not.

the students who take it do better than average! (If you didn't get that joke, you're in trouble with basic statistics.) Most universities require that you take this at some point in your high school career, but unlike some of the other tests, you can take the SAT a couple of times to try to improve your score. Many high schools urge students to take it at the end of their junior year.

The test consists of three math sections and three verbal sections, as well as a set of practice questions, and takes up three full hours of your Saturday morning (plus breaks) that you would have otherwise spent sleeping. The math sections are divided into basic problem solving and "quantitative comparisons," where they give you two values and you have to say which is larger. The test tries to gauge if you can think in the way they want you to and isn't about seeing if you remember how to do long division, so you'll be allowed to use a calculator.

The verbal sections are divided into three parts: sentence completions, which are essentially Mad Libs with only one correct answer; analogies, which ask you to compare relationships between two things; and critical reading passages, which demand that you answer questions about a short, often boring essay or story. Although the SAT claims to test only your "verbal reasoning abilities," implicit in this promulgation is that you apprehend the prerequisite erudition of the lexicon. In other words, you'll have to learn a lot of vocabulary words that no one ever uses.

As you probably know, aside from a few math questions, you answer all the questions by filling in tiny bubbles. Once you've finished taking the test, your test is sent back to the mysterious

The first SAT was administered on June 23, 1926. Developed by Princeton academic Carl Campbell Brigham, the test favored knowledge of baseball games and cuts of beef over strategy and comprehension.

Princeton, NJ stronghold that is Educational Testing Services, where your test is scored and your results normalized onto a scale of 200 to 1600. Your results are sent back to you in three to five weeks, although it will feel like five to seven weeks. As with all standardized tests, keep in mind that your score doesn't really reflect how smart you are, but how good you are at taking that standardized test, which itself tested only a few particular skills. That should explain why your friend, who keeps flaunting his 1410, is barely passing history.

Why Should I Take the SAT?

Since the SAT is designed to test reasoning abilities independent of the things you learn in class, colleges use it (along with your GPA, class rank, and advice from Miss Cleo's Psychic Network) as a way to predict how well you'll do at their school. The test is losing favor as of late, however, as statistical analyses have shown that it doesn't do this as well as your GPA, your class rank, or Miss Cleo's prognoses. As of August 2001, 388 out of 1,788 American colleges and universities don't require SAT scores from all applicants. No joke! This includes schools like Bates, Bowdoin, Connecticut, Dickinson, Franklin & Marshall, Middlebury, Mount Holyoke, Texas, UC Berkeley, and UCLA! Pretty awesome, right?

Actually, not really. Chances are at least one school you'll want to apply to will demand to see the fruits of your prep course labors. Besides, of the 383 schools that don't require it, most will still accept it, so you might as well suck it up and give it a go, because a good score will only help your chances. Some colleges even give course placement for high scores.

To sum up, if you want to go to college and there's only one test you plan on taking, it might as well be the SAT. Just keep in mind that even a sweet 1600 won't help you that much if you fail all your other classes because you don't take any other tests.

The PSAT/NMSQT: The Biggie Lite

In addition to having an unnecessarily long name, the Preliminary SAT/National Merit Scholarship Qualifying Test gives students a chance to get their feet wet in the bubbly waters of the standardized test lake. Colleges don't look at how you did on this test, but that doesn't mean you should just try to make pretty zigzag patterns on your answer sheet. As well as helping you prepare

The average lead pencil will draw a line 35 miles long or write approximately 50,000 English words. More than 2 billion pencils are manufactured in the U.S. annually. If these were laid end to end, they would circle the earth nine times.

Source:
www.qualitymag.com

for the SAT, the PSAT is used in a national scholarship competition. The PSAT is offered only once a year in October, and while some schools allow sophomores to take it as practice, you'll probably take it for real as a junior.

If the SAT and the SAT II Writing test (see SAT IIs) had a baby, it would likely resemble the PSAT. Clocking in at a somewhat more manageable two hours and ten minutes, the PSAT has two verbal sections, two math sections (both of which contain a handful of actual SAT questions), and a writing skills section. Your results are converted onto a 240-point scale consisting of 80 points for each subject. Probably the most important thing you get from your scores is knowing what subjects you are weak in, so you'll know whether you need to make flashcards for vocabulary words or for math things in preparing for the biggie.

Why Should I Take the PSAT?

Of the 1.2 million students who take the PSAT every fall, the 50,000 or so with the highest composite scores get official recognition from the National Merit people. This in itself is kind of cool, since it's another important-sounding achievement you can put on your important-sounding achievements list that all colleges ask for. Of the 50,000, about 7,900 win big scholarships after advancing through a series of rounds that take longer than a year-and-a-half to complete for some inexplicable reason. If you are in a position to take the PSAT, you probably should. Even if you don't think you have a real shot at winning a scholarship, you might surprise yourself, and either way you'll get a taste of what taking the SAT is like.

The ACT: The Biggie's Cousin from the Midwest

Developed at the University of Iowa, the American College Testing Assessment Test is required by some colleges, and accepted at nearly all. It differs from the SAT in that it tests knowledge of the sciences as well as math, and splits English and reading into two different sections. In general, it tests your memory of things that you have learned in class, rather than reasoning methods you learn specifically in SAT prep courses—but this is not a hard and fast rule. Like the SAT, it's offered several times a year and you are encouraged to take it more than once to improve your score, which is normalized on a 1–36 point scale.

The English section tests punctuation, grammar, sentence structure, and rhetorical strategy, organization, and style. This may seem like a lot of material, and it is, but there are not as many questions that require that you know the definitions of words like "abstemious" and "octogenarian." The reading section simply asks you questions about passages taken from the natural and social sciences, as well as the humanities and even some delightful prose fiction.

The science section requires a background in biology, chemistry, physics, geology, astronomy, and meteorology—basically all the sciences there are. Don't be too intimidated though, since you won't be asked to recall the half-life of Uranium 238 or anything (although in case you are, it's 4.5 billion years). Instead, most of the questions will involve reading data off charts and analyzing experiments. Finally, the math section, which takes up the most time of all the sections, covers slightly more material than the SAT does, dipping into the scary realm of trigonometry.

Why Should I Take the ACT?

The reasons why you should take the ACT are essentially the same as for why you should take the SAT: because "the man" says so. Colleges will want to see how you compare with other people on a standard test of knowledge, and the SAT and ACT are just the conventional tests people have used for years.

Because the ACT tests very different skills than does the SAT, and most colleges are now willing to accept either, it may be to your advantage to decide which is more likely to showcase your particular talents. This chart outlines the major differences between the two. Keep in mind, however, that it may be best just to take both and only submit the scores of the one you did better on.

The ACT	The SAT
Includes a section on science.	Friendly to those who are bad at science.
The math section contains trigonometry questions.	Friendly to those who are bad at trigonometry.
The authors of the questions in the reading and English sections do not go out of their way to frustrate you with obscure vocabulary.	The authors of the questions in the verbal sections think obscure vocabulary is A.O.K. to test.
The English section tests basic grammar (punctuation, etc.).	Friendly to those who are bad at grammar.

The PLAN: The Biggie's Cousin from the Midwest Lite

Here's a practice analogy for you: The SAT is to the PSAT as the ACT is to the ___? You guessed it, my friend! The PLAN is usually taken in the fall of your sophomore year as a "pre-ACT"; the content essentially mirrors that of the ACT. In addition to letting you know what to expect from the ACT, the PLAN also contains an extensive section that collects data about your interests so a computer program in Iowa can spit out information about your career options and scholarship opportunities. While it is unclear just how useful this information is (you don't hear that many stories about people getting their information sheet and then deciding to become a veterinarian all of a sudden), it's usually better to know more about your choices than less.

Why Should I Take the PLAN?

Unlike the PSAT, scoring well will not put you in the running for the National Merit Scholarship. However, if you're planning on taking the ACT, you might as well give it a shot so you know where you stand. (As you may have noticed by now, we tend to support taking most standardized tests.)

The SAT II: The Half-Brother of the Biggie

Want to take a standardized test to show off your knowledge of U.S. History, Chemistry, German, German with Listening, Math IIC, or any of the other 22 subject areas tested by the Scholastic Aptitude Test II? Then the SAT II might be the test for you! Each exam is only one hour long, and unlike the tests described above, the SAT II tests your knowledge in only one subject. Awesome, huh? The subjects offered cover English, history, math, science and several foreign languages. It's usually best to take the SAT II right after you've finished a class on a given subject, but we guess that's kind of obvious. Much like the section of the SAT I, each test you take is scored on a scale of 200–800.

A number of schools ask that you take a couple different SAT IIs so they can see how you compare with the other students in the admissions pool on a standard test of straight-fact knowledge. Probably the most important of these is the SAT II in Writing, which some schools outright require. This test consists of a series of multiple choice questions regarding grammar and sentence structure, and is capped off with a 20-minute essay, which is graded by hand. The essay questions generally ask you to agree or disagree with a statement like "Silence is the most effective tool of argument" using any example that you'd like, so feel free to talk about things that happened to you when you were a kid. Or you can lie and use things that you pretend happened to you when you were a kid even though they didn't, because they'll have no way of knowing. Or you can just talk about Gandhi; pretty much anything is fine.

Why should I take the SAT II?

Many schools require or recommend that you submit one to three SAT II scores along with your application, and in order to get the scores, you'll have to take the tests. As mentioned above, you should probably take Writing for sure. A lot of students take the Math IC or Math IIC and a language that they have taken for several years, since they test things that you've been studying for a while. Similarly, a lot of schools accept high scores on these tests for course placement or even credit, so depending on your situation, it might even be worth taking them after you've already been accepted to college. The bottom line, however, is that you should take the ones in the subjects you know best.

The AP Exams: The Big Brother of the Half-Brother of the Biggie

AP (Advanced Placement) tests are taken by thousands of students each May upon the completion of AP-level courses. Designed to cover the academic breadth of a college course (but without the horrible dorm food), each AP course goes into greater detail and analysis than most of the courses at your high school probably do. This means that the AP Spanish Language test will probably be a lot harder than Señora Waldman's Spanish III final—if for no other reason than because it takes three hours! Tests are normalized onto a scale of 1–5, and while you may retake specific tests, colleges will receive both scores. Of all the tests described in this section, this one has the most ramifications for your actual college career, with many colleges accepting AP scores for college placement or credit. That's why so many seniors take them even after they're accepted to college.

Some high schools allow you to take an AP-level class without taking the AP test. Similarly, if your high school does not offer an AP class in a subject that you already have a strong background in, if you talk with your guidance counselor, you will probably be able to take the test anyway.

Should I Take Any AP Exams?

Of all the tests we've gone over so far, the AP exams are the most like gravy on the application steak. AP tests are hard, but doing well on them is a nice ace to have up your sleeve. AP courses are supposed to cover the range of material covered in college courses, so taking one or more might cause you to go insane, depending on your situation. If your school offers AP courses, ask your guidance counselor whether you should take them, and if your school doesn't, ask your guidance counselor if it would be worth your while to find a way to take them. In either case, simply ask your guidance counselor how he or she is doing every morning to build a rewarding lifelong friendship.

The TOEFL: The Foreign Exchange Student Living with the Biggie

The Test of English as a Foreign Language is required of non-native speakers (mainly international students) for over 2,400 colleges. Of all the tests, the TOEFL is definitely the most "twenty-first century," in that you can take it from a computer. The computer-based test consists of four sections (listening, structure, reading, and writing). The paper-and-pencil test, which is offered where computer testing is sadly unavailable, is similarly structured, but instead of a writing section, students have to take a separate test with a separate abbreviation (the Test of Written English, or TWE).

Why Should I Take the TOEFL?

If you are a non-native, or if English is your second language, you will almost definitely have to take this test because most schools have a minimum score (550) that you have to reach before they'll accept you. Sorry!

A dark day in high school student history: On December 19, 1947, ETS received a non-profit charter and officially came into existence. Before that date you didn't need SAT scores to get into college.

Where/When/How Do I Take All These Tests?

All right, so now you're all psyched and ready to kick some standardized butt. Before you can start kicking, however, you've got to jump through some hoops, and there are a few logistical details you should be keen to as well. Ergo, this chapter. While each test has its own specific lowdown, most are conducted in about the same way; we'll use the SAT as our template.

Your first step will be to find out when the test you want to take is offered (ask your guidance counselor) and then register before a given deadline. Registration is a very straightforward process that involves filling out a form and giving someone some money. You can register for the SAT on the web now from the College Board's website (www.

collegeboard.com), but chances are that your guidance counselor will have you fill out a paper form so he can send out all the registration material for your school at one time. He's compulsive like that.

When you register, be sure to let them know if you need to take advantage of their Sunday morning test option (if you have a religious observance to attend to) or if you need disability assistance (see below). Incidentally, if you're too busy cramming for your French midterm and you forget to register, you might be able to register late, or even take the test stand-by. If you try to do this, call the test center ahead of time and sound as apologetic as you can when you ask if they will have an extra test for you, and hope that they'll have some pity on you. Incidentally, if you accidentally register for a test and then find out you can't make it because your

ETS sent out over 1,500 letters to students who took the SAT I in May of 1999, explaining that due to scoring error, their scores may have been reported 50-100 points lower. At least they had a score, unlike the 650 California students who had to retake the exam when Federal Express lost their scores.

Source: www.fairtest.org

football team pulled the upset and made it to States and you can't miss the big game, you can also call them to reregister—which you should—so that those pathetic-sounding stand-by's have a chance.

Registration is also the time to let the testing people know if you will need accommodations for a disability. Most tests have extended time options, and you can get tests in Braille or enlarged fonts, people to help you transcribe answers, and a number of other aids, so if there's anything that could help you take the test more fairly (a smart person on a leash does not count as a seeing-eye dog, by the way), go ahead and ask; it can't hurt!

As mentioned above, you have to pay each time you want to take the test. Taking the SAT (or ACT) costs $24 (which includes the cost of having your scores sent to a few schools or scholarship programs), but the prices vary greatly from test to test. While you can take some of the SAT II subject tests for as little as $6 (enough to buy a few nice pairs of socks),[1] the AP exams carry a mightier $77 price tag (enough to buy a nice pair of basketball sneakers or a few pairs of *really* nice socks).

Don't panic, however, as registration fee waivers are available for students who cannot easily afford the test fees. The waivers cover the $13 registration fee of the SAT, in addition to the cost of an automated "question and answer service" that gives you a detailed breakdown of your performance. To apply, ask your

---

1. This is on top of a $13 basic registration fee; once you've paid that, some of the SAT II tests are $6 each.

guidance counselor for contact information for your nearest College Board Regional Office. Similar fee waivers are available for the other tests, including a nearly identical waiver system for the ACT. Some federal and state funding is even available for the costly AP tests; for regional information, check out the College Board's state initiative website at www.collegeboard.org/ap/stateinit.

When the day of the test arrives, you'll have to show up at the test location *early* in the morning, so you may not want to go to that big "Anything Goes" cast party the night before the test. The SAT, for example, is given at 8:3o A.M. on a Saturday. Other tests, such as some of the AP exams, are given in the afternoon. Your guidance counselor, always a wonderful source of information, will let you know the testing location ahead of time.

The SAT-prep industry—including classes, private tutors, online help, books, videos, and computer programs—pulls in about $200 million a year.

It'll probably be a local high school, perhaps your crosstown rivals. If, however, the nearest testing location is a not-so-local high school (i.e. more than 75 miles away), you can write a letter to ETS ahead of time and they will try to set up something closer for you.

Don't forget to bring stuff with you! You'll need to tote along your admission ticket (which you'll receive in the mail upon registering), "acceptable" identification such as your driver's license (don't show them your fake ID by mistake!), a calculator if you're taking a test that requires a calculator, a ton of #2 pencils, and your brain, which by this point should be saturated with useless pieces of knowledge. That's basically all you need.

A few weeks after the test, you'll get your scores in the mail along with brochures from all the colleges who have been courting you for the last few months. If you can't wait the extra few days for the scores to arrive, you can check your scores over the phone. There's a section on the test that asks you to name the colleges and scholarship programs to which you'd like your scores sent out; they'll all get them about when you do. If you got lucky on all the questions you guessed on and want even more schools and programs to see your phat verbal count, you can make it happen by either mailing a form out or by going to the College Board's website. If you took the SAT II and had your scores placed on hold so you'd know which tests you did best on, don't forget to release them. Finally, if you think you did better than the numbers claim, you can have your test regraded by hand, but don't expect any miracles.

Preparing for Standardized Tests

All right, enough of this. Let's get to the main attraction of this chapter: the secrets that all but guarantee you'll get a 1600 on any test (and that includes the ACT, whose grading scale only goes up to 36!). We've divided the tips into general advice about how you should approach the tests and more specific advice for when you're actually taking them. Kick it, dawg!

Approaching the Tests

(1) Know exactly what's going to be on the test. This goes for both directions and content. There's really no excuse for spending valuable question-answering time reading directions that you should already know, and there's even less than no excuse for learning halfway through the test that familiarity with the works of Gabriel Garcia Marquez is required for the AP Spanish Literature exam. This is the most obvious piece of advice we could give you, but it's still important.

(2) To master the test format—and simply to feel comfortable when you're in the hot seat—you should take as many practice tests as possible. Entire bookfuls of old SATs are out there, and you shouldn't have trouble finding at least practice questions for all the other exams. Don't forget about the PSAT and PLAN (as if you could!). A lot of questions you'll encounter on the tests you actually take will seem much more familiar and will probably require the exact same math formulas or use the same esoteric

Resist your temptation to hire someone to take the SAT for you—according to a 1992 *New York Times* article, a student who tried to do this was arrested and charged with criminal perjury.

vocabulary words as those on your practice test, so learn how to answer each question correctly. This is the second most obvious piece of advice we could give you.

(3) A lot of tests—such as the SAT verbal section and most SAT II subjects tests and AP exams—demand a lot of strict memorization. Memorizing things is very tedious and not fun, but is nevertheless something you just can't get around doing. Come up with some sort of system that works for you, like using those vocabulary cards your mom bought you. Just make sure that you're learning the right stuff—don't waste time learning bizarre French words when the ones that show up on your AP French Language exam are common vernacular.

(4) Read as much as you can in your spare time to both expand your vocabulary and to tickle your imagination with the fantastic

company of Pippi Longstocking and Ivan Denisovich. This holds especially true if you're studying for a foreign language exam. Books that are particularly useful in preparing for standardized tests include this one and many of the other fine books written by Harvard Student Agencies.

(5) If your test has a free-response essay section, think of particular topics or works you'd like to write about ahead of time. There's no guarantee that you'll be able to use any of the ideas from your pre-test brainstorming session, but there is a chance. For example, the SAT II Writing test lets you write about things that have happened to you in your life or things in popular culture, so look through your old diaries and back issues of *Rolling Stone*. It's never a bad decision to write about Gandhi.

(6) At the end of the twentieth century, mankind witnessed a technological revolution that can only be described as "totally ginormous." The epitome of this revolution is the availability of test prep software packages. Some of these babies do a pretty fabulous job of pinpointing your weaknesses and giving you exercises to improve your score. If you are in a position to get your hands on the useful diagnostic and teaching tools that these fancy computer programs offer, we would strongly recommend giving them a try.

(7) On a related note, the Internet has a lot of test-taking resources for you to explore. There are plenty of message boards and newsgroups, such as soc.college.admissions, that discuss further general test-taking strategies. Also keep your eyes peeled for

"Go to the bathroom before you start the test. I can't stress this enough!"
–Senior, University of Pennsylvania

"Everyone says that the ACT is a big deal, but it's just a test. Unlike normal tests, you can even take it more than once if you do badly!"
–Sophomore, Marquette University

"I'm really glad I took the SAT again my senior fall. I kind of didn't want to, but I ended up doing 80 points better than the last time."
–Junior, Cornell University

sites that specialize in specific things, such as vocabulary building. The College Board website, www.collegeboard.org, features an "SAT Question of the Day" section that just might help you raise your score by 100 points or so.

(8) If you're really lucky, you might have the opportunity to have your parents involuntarily enroll you in a test-prep class. Students tend to say these are actually pretty helpful, so look around for them in your area if you can.

(9) A lot of people (at least four) will tell you that it's important to get a good night's sleep and eat well the morning of your test. This is generally good advice for all situations. Just be sure to use your own judgment—if getting too much sleep makes you tired and lethargic the following morning, don't go nuts and binge on sleep the night before the big test.

(10) In general, a lot of other sources of information on test-taking strategies you may encounter tend to speak in terms of absolutes: *"never* cram the night before a test" or "learn ten new vocabulary words *every day*." Again, use your judgment—if you only passed Mr. Johnson's bio midterm because you crammed the night before, don't rule out studying the night before the SAT II Biology test. Similarly, it may be humanly impossible to learn ten new vocabulary words every day.

Taking the Tests

(1) Almost all standardized tests put all the easy questions before the harder ones, we suppose so that you'll be warmed up by the time you get to the impossible questions. At any rate, definitely answer the easier questions first—they're worth just as much as the hard questions (on most tests). Just make sure not to skim over them; you'll feel awful if you leave the test and realize that you said that Denzel Washington was our nation's first president.

(2) Know when to guess on multiple-choice questions! Different tests score differently, but in general, if you can eliminate two or more choices, you will statistically perform better if you guess. Sure, there's a penalty for guessing wrong, but if you lose a fourth of a point for each guess, and you narrow it down from five choices to three on three separate questions, you'll probably get one right and your net score will be +.5 points instead of zero. Anyway, you get the idea.

(3) Don't get too hung up on any one problem, and don't be afraid to leave a question blank if you really have no idea which answer is right. There are so many question-fish in the standardized-test sea, and it really is better to get through as much of the test as possible. Besides, this isn't a Grand Jury trial or anything—one question won't really make that much of a difference.

(4) Don't be afraid to mark up the test booklets by underlining important parts of reading passages, circling questions you have to go back to, or drawing ugly diagrams for math problems. Remember that you're not taking the SAT II Figure Drawing test, so style and neatness count for nothing. They're only going to look at your answer sheet. Which, incidentally, should be *impeccably clean!* Seriously, fill in your answer sheet carefully and avoid making stray marks that will cause the Scantron program to explode.

(5) For multiple-choice questions, look over the possible answers closely, especially for math problems. It might be more efficient to just substitute each of the answers into the equation or what have you to see which value holds true, and work backwards that way. For other types of questions, however, such as sentence completions, it may be better to try to think of the answers before polluting your mind with the choices. Try different strategies on practice tests, and see what works for you.

(6) Some will advise you to work as quickly and efficiently as you can, to try to get through all the problems on the test. Others will tell you to spend a lot of time on each question so you make sure

that you get the ones you answer right. Our advice? Do both of these things. There's definitely a tension here; you'll probably only find the rate of answering questions at which you're most successful by taking practice tests. It might be a good idea to try to take a practice test without timing yourself, and then another with the actual time limit, so you can find the right balance for you.

(7) If on any multiple-choice question two of the answers are exactly equivalent (for example, two different choices are words that are literal synonyms, or the two are mathematical values that are equal), cross them off as choices. They can't *both* be right, after all! Be careful though to make sure that the choices are identical and not just merely similar, or you might find yourself making a big mistake.

(8) If you're taking a test with essay questions, know what the graders want from your essay. For example, on the AP Biology exam, the graders will simply be looking to see how many facts about marine life you drop into your sentences, and care little about your style of writing. In contrast, the graders for the SAT II Writing exam will simply be looking for how clearly you can construct an argument and write, and any fact about marine life you include will just be gravy.

(9) Knowing what the question is asking isn't the same as giving the correct answer. For your AP History exam, make sure you answer the essay question and don't just talk about why you think James K. Polk was the best president ever, even if the question is

about a time period when he was president. Similarly, if a math question asks you to solve for x+2, once you know what x is, be sure to add 2.

(10) In general, just try to keep your brain alive while you take the test. Pay attention, stay alert, and be careful. Read each question slowly so you don't have to look over it again, and try to keep your mind from dozing off. Taking the ACT is the wrong time to practice your Zen meditation. Be one with the *test*, not the back of your eyelids.

The take-home message for this chapter is that standardized tests do, in fact, exist. Not only that, but you'll almost certainly have to take at least a couple. Now that you've heard our piece, hopefully when your opponent challenges you for using terms like "TOEFL" and "NMSQT" in your next Scrabble game, you'll be able to tell her more than she'd ever want to hear about these essential exams. The bottom line, however, is that standardized tests are just another unfortunate obstacle you have to, but can, deal with on your way to higher education. Study and take them seriously, but don't worry that your favorite school won't accept you because you got a few points lower than the mean score of all the students they accept—remember, half the students did worse than that. Good luck—you'll need it! (Especially on multiple-choice questions #24-27 of your AP English exam next spring—who the heck knows what a synecdoche is anyway?)

CHAPTER THREE

First, They Hunt You and Then, You Hunt Them...

Starting Out in the College Search Game

You've always wanted to be a celebrity, right? From the end of your sophomore to the middle of your senior year in high school, you will be—at least in the eyes of colleges—the coolest being to walk the planet since Michael Jackson (in the early days, at least). You represent thousands of dollars worth of tuition to these places of higher learning and they'll woo you with everything they can think of: brochures, free CDs, brochures, elaborate websites, brochures, wall posters, and plenty of brochures. If you've also managed to distinguish yourself on the PSAT or another stan-dardized test, you're even more valuable. Not only are you likely to be a bright student, but you also represent a chance for a school to pull up its average test scores or increase its number of National Merit Scholars by one. Essentially, your scores are bragging rights for them.

A wee bit cynical? Sure. But colleges need to sell themselves in the same way that soft drink companies and car dealerships do; in other words, you'll be getting only one side of the story. If you passively sit back and choose the school with the nicest pamphlet or the most flattering letter, it may lead to trouble (if for no other reason than you'll have to choose between dozens). Organizing and evaluating the deluge of letters and the preponderance of books and websites that rate, rank, and recommend schools is a daunting task, but one that will pay huge dividends in helping you make an informed decision.

The stretch of eighteen months from the start of your junior to the middle of your senior year is a time for you to actively build a list of colleges that interest you. Maybe the undergraduate research program described in one of those mass-mailings caught your eye. Maybe a cousin's description of the social life at her alma mater makes you salivate. Maybe you're interested in finding a school that's tops in art or engineering. No matter how specific or nonexistent your criteria are, there are a few things for any potential applicant to keep in mind—whether you're a future geologist or graphic designer, applying to the Ivy Leagues or to the place down the street.

Most important of all, you should sit back, relax, and enjoy the attention—you have enough time left to savor high school and (we hope) enough initiative to begin the search for what comes next without drowning in the deluge of colorful brochures already arriving in your mailbox.

Organize Thyself

On the PSAT or the SAT or the ACT or any of those standardized tests with an acronym for a name, hidden below the demographic questions is a little box that says, "Check here if you'd like colleges to send you information." And, not thinking, you probably have checked or will check that box. Doing so has consequences—not bad ones, but ones you should be aware of.

The major consequence is the flood of mail you will receive. Ask any mail carrier, they know who in town is thinking about college. Colleges can't wait to advertise. After all, you're not just a prospective student, you're a pro-

If you're the sort of person who does things because other people do them, then you should seriously think about going to college. In 1997, 67 percent of high school graduates went directly to college—70 percent of the females and 64 percent of the males.

Source:
www.idahoea.org

spective tuition bill. Taking any of those standardized tests is like declaring your eligibility for the NBA draft, except without the million-dollar contracts and limousine rides.

Even if you haven't taken one of these tests, colleges have apparently taken lessons from telemarketers—no one is safe.

It's kind of cool. You can impress your parents and relatives. "Look Mom, I *am* a good student: I got three letters from the University of Puget Sound in one week! They really want me." Your pacifist flute player friend will get deluged by ROTC recruiting info. Women's colleges will occasionally screw up and send letters to guys. Weird stuff goes down.

Pretty soon the literature is so piled up it gets hard to move around your house. There are two knee-jerk reactions to this correspondence, neither of which will help you much in the long run:

1. ANSWER THEM ALL. Oh such a tempting option when those first few gems come through! But as a starry-eyed sophomore, you can't help but feel flattered when a college sends you a letter with a little reply card tucked inside. You quickly fill it out, complete with middle initial and home phone number. The next week you get two reply cards. The next week four. Then eight. After ten weeks, you're getting 1,024 reply cards (recall exponential growth from your algebra class). You are under no obligation to reply to these guys and under no obligation to provide them with information you feel uncomfortable sending out to strangers (e.g. your social security number). Which is not to say you should simply resort to the second approach ...

2. TOSS 'EM OUT. Yeah you'll reach that point soon enough. Easiest thing to do with a pile of stuff is just to toss it out, no questions asked. But you'll be losing potentially valuable information if you do this, especially if you inadvertently trash materials from a school you're interested in and lose information from other schools that may have intrigued you. That, and think of all those trees that died so that Juniata College could send you three beautifully colored postcards about their lovely school.

So you need to get organized. You'll need a large box, paper bag, or one of those neat expandable file folders—something you can neatly stack papers in. Organization works best when you do it a little bit at a time (despite the teenage credo of persistent procrastination). If you take care of those letters every couple of days, you'll stay ahead of the game.

What exactly does "taking care of them" consist of? For starters, junk the ones you are certain you have no interest in. Small college in Wyoming not your style? Junk it. Military academy just not you? Junk it. Place that doesn't offer the major you're absolutely in love with since the second grade? Junk it.

There's a fine line between indifference and not interested. Don't agonize over throwing out brochures; colleges will be glad to send you more if you write or email them. In general, though, everything is worth a quick glance. Among the unknowns you may find a college or two that has a unique system for educating its students or finding them jobs. Maybe a couple schools will offer you attractive and guaranteed financial aid packages. As you develop a list of criteria for a college, you may stumble across one

The seven cities with the most college students are New York, Los Angeles, Chicago, San Francisco, Boston, Washington DC, and Philadelphia.
Source: The Philadelphia Business Journal

that matches up well with the size, location, courses, and reputation you were hoping to find. Hopefully, you'll find *something* worth at least a second look.

This is where that folder or box comes in. Go ahead and toss in those second-lookers, after giving your parents a chance to ogle the latest offering from the world of higher education. Generally it's also a good idea to organize your materials—alphabetically works well, but pick a system that makes sense to you (regional, desirability, chaos theory, etc.).

From this group, there will undoubtedly be a few that you think are really cool. Always wanted to go to Hollywood Upstairs University and they sent you an app? The school that's tops in the country for accounting wants you and you actually want to be an accountant? Great! These are the ones you want to set aside. If you know you are interested in a college or were interested even before you got the application or know for sure you want to apply, these schools get a sub folder (or a shoebox inside the refrigerator box). You may also want to keep a running list of these top choices. This will help you to focus your attention on a few places and gather supplemental information from websites, books, and the occasional field trip to the campus. If one of those second-lookers is growing on you, feel free to add it to the list.

By the end of your junior year, this list will probably be nearing its final form. Feel free to add last-minute candidates as you like and don't hesitate to knock a school off if you can't for the life of you remember what you saw in it. If you keep those old flyers boxed, you can even revisit a couple of them occasionally to make sure you haven't remembered your top choice as being in a dif-

According to the Department of Labor, employment in the food service industry in the United States will increase by 32 percent by 2005.

Source: U.S. Department of Labor, Bureau of Labor Statistics

ferent state or come to the crushing realization that the university all your friends are going to just doesn't have that geology program, which you need more than life itself (lets face it folks, tectonic plates can be just that compelling).

Toss what you don't want and keep what you do want. Organize what you keep. Start to look into the ones you like. If for no other reason, keep this stuff around so that you can daydream about a world with no Physical Education, and classes that start in the afternoon.

Whaddaya Want?

Time to turn the tables. Just as colleges have lots of hard-to-quantify criteria they look for in students, you now have the chance to rule out certain colleges based on your own set of preferences. There's no single list of personal criteria that's right for everyone and it's perfectly acceptable for the attributes you find most important to your happiness and education to change over time.

The list of ideas here is meant to give you a jumping off point and is by no means all-inclusive or sacred. Conversely, you will want to give at least a passing thought to most of these:

1. Location, Location, Location

The mantra of real estate can become the mantra of a college applicant as well. Location is hopefully not the make-it-or-break-it factor in adding a university to your short list, but it's more important than most people give it credit for.

Location can mean something as simple as the weather. As a Hawaiian famously remarked on a beautiful fifteen-degree Boston morning his freshman year, "What happened? Is the sun broken?" An Arizonan who moved to Boston made the opposite mistake, showing up in August with a suitcase full of sweaters and a parka. He sweltered in 80-degree weather for the next two months. What we're saying is know what you're getting yourself into. People are constantly moaning about the weather and just once, we'd like to hear someone say, "Why yes, I did realize and thoughtfully considered that there would be no sunlight in this godforsaken place for weeks on end, but, darnit, it's worth it." We'll keep dreaming.

Think about location for more important reasons, too. Obviously if you're living 1,000 miles from home you won't be coming home on a regular basis. Not only do you miss out on Mom's homemade chocolate chip cookies, but you're away from old friends and family. This is hard under the best of circumstances. College is not the best of circumstances. If you just broke up with your significant other or got your butt kicked by an exam or got chewed out by your RA for that game of floor hockey you just *had* to play in the hall, your old support structure is not there to help you out. The Internet has made staying in touch—via e-mail and Instant Messenger—easier than ever before, but sometimes there's no substitute for the real thing. Your little brother bouncing a baseball off the back of your head can have an effect far more powerful than a long distance phone call.

In spite of these drawbacks, the freedom of living far from home is a powerful and dynamic force in the life of a young person. Losing your keys or losing a button off your shirt means suddenly the problem is yours to solve. This is vexing but also liberating. Either you learn to sew (or find a friend who knows how) or you go around with dilapidated clothing. Your life is, more than ever before, in your own hands. As most of the remainder of your life will be lived in this fashion, it's not a bad idea to begin taking over your own laundry, meals, and budgeting sooner rather than later.

Maybe it's too soon. There's nothing wrong with living close to home or even at home during your college years. You'll save money on travel, your support system will be relatively intact, and Mom can make her deservedly famous lasagna for you on Thursday nights. You may even retain a fair amount of privacy and independence if you explain to your parents that even though you only live a half-hour away, they shouldn't be expecting to drop in on a moment's notice for a Friday night game of canasta. Manage to do this and you'll have the best of both worlds.

Friends will put you in a similarly awkward dilemma when it comes to the question of distance. Go to the local college with a couple of buds from high school and you'll never go lonely on a Saturday night. But, you may also miss out on thousands of cool new people because you're chilling with your high school pals. This is another situation where you need to know what suits your personality best. If you're adept at meeting new people while maintaining ties with your old friends, going to school with or near a bunch of high school friends isn't a bad idea. If you think they will monopolize your time or that you're so wrapped up with them that you have no need or desire to branch out, it may be time to strike out on your own. High school is capable of producing wonderful, lifelong relationships, but the hard truth is that people change tremendously during college. If you are basing your top-choice college solely upon where your best friend or friends are going, take a long time and try to come up with at least one other compelling reason to apply.

2. Academics

Oh, what, you thought we'd forget about this? No way buddy, this is why you're going to college (mostly).

If you have definite ideas about what you want to study, then making sure a school has that major and—a strong reputation is a, if not *the*, top priority. There is nothing more tragic than arriving on campus the first day and realizing that there *is* no astronomy program, or that the computer lab that is supposed to serve 30,000 undergrads is actually a couple dozen beat up old Power Macs, and you can't possibly be a computer scientist under those conditions. Maybe the creative writing class you want to take only allows twelve people in, there are 300 applicants, and they didn't like your poems about licorice from your summer at writers' camp. (Harvard applicants beware of this one.) Suddenly you might really wish you had gone some place else. Make sure your college will allow you to follow your dreams.

Don't think you have to give up on big name schools to study fashion: Cornell University offers undergraduate and graduate degrees in apparel design, apparel and textile management, and fiber science.

Browse through the college's website, check out sites from individual departments for class listings and prereqs or write them for more information. You may even be able to find an administrator, professor, or student willing to take a few minutes to explain the unique facets of their particular program to you. There's no substitute for firsthand (if slightly biased) information.

A word of caution on majors: *everybody* changes their minds. Everybody. Even the guy who said he wanted to be a biologist in third grade, and then said it each year after, then majored in biology, and then went on to get a Ph.D in biology changed his mind at some point. He went from liking birds to seagulls or from cell biology to microbiology, but he learned something new at some point that really excited him, or there was a mentor at some point who forced him to think in a new way or a lab that changed the way he imagined chemicals, and he decided to concentrate on one of those things.

So lets say you've sought out and found the top university in the nation for undergraduate education in neonatal equine pre-veterinary sciences—that's right, you want to be a pony doctor when you grow up. You may even beat the odds and stick with it the whole way through. But what if you don't? What if during your freshman year you take a math class that fascinates you, volunteer at a school and decide your true calling is teaching, or you get abducted by aliens and decide that hunting them shall be your life's work? Does your school even offer classes in math, education, or parapsychology? If you are already wavering and there are simply dozens upon dozens of things that interest you,

Looking to meet lots of new people? Ohio State boasts a whopping enrollment of just over 55,000 students as of Autumn 2001.

you would probably be better served by a larger school or at the very least one that will let you switch majors easily.

Again, there's no need to wed yourself to one course of action at this early date. But find out what schools will allow you to do the things you love (or think you love or think you might love if your top choice doesn't work out). And things you love might also include . . .

3. Extracurricular Activities

Do they have a choir (or two or three or eight)? You want to walk onto their NCAA Division III Swim team after an illustrious high school career, but do they have a pool? If your jump shot is not everything you'd once hoped it would be, can you join an intramural team? If your drumming is merely adequate, is the marching band completely desperate for anyone who can walk and beat things at the same time?

Extracurriculars are likely the place where you spent a lot of time in high school and where you met a lot of your closest friends. The same is true in college. If for whatever reason a particular university is down on student groups or the students at a school just don't seem to be interested in doing much, you should be aware of it. You can always go charging in and start your own student organization (you rebel, you!), but keep in mind what you're in for in the extracurricular department.

Extracurriculars also include socializing—and that's not limited to parties either. There are thousands of people from new states and different countries who will challenge you, agree with you, fall in love with you, play bad music really loudly at one in the morning across the hall from you, and basically interact with you in every way that two human beings can interact with each other. This happens at every college and has an undeniable and deep impact on your outlook on life. There are numerous publications that purport to measure how happy and socially active students are. The guidebooks are nice and even if they tend to overgeneralize, you'll at least know that many of the individuals at your school spend nine hours a night studying, so you're not likely to hook up with your dream guy from Texas at a beer-chugging party. Of course there are plenty of other schools where frats are where it's at or where all the RAs seem to inevitably disappear on Friday night, leading to mass carnage. These institutions may make it hard to discuss the meaning of life with

Afraid of meeting too many new people? Then the school for you just might be Deep Springs College in California, with only 26 students per undergraduate class. All 26 are male, however, so if you're looking for ladies, look elsewhere!

that girl from philosophy section and are less than . . . HEY KEEP IT DOWN!!! . . . are less than ideal for . . . I SWEAR TO GOD, I'M CALLING THE COPS IF YOU DON'T QUIET DOWN!!! . . . are less than ideal for . . . SERIOUSLY, PEOPLE!!! . . . less than ideal for getting your work done.

Hopefully you don't want it just one way or the other. Most colleges agree and try to make sure you have the chance to do a little of each.

Even if you're a commuter or planning on working forty hours a week, you might still find a lecture series or pottery classes on Sunday that you'd like to attend, so don't ignore opportunities outside of the classroom entirely.

College is more than just school, so make sure that you can pursue activities and people in a manner (fast, furious, and wild; mysterious, intelligent, and quiet; or somewhere in between) that matches your own style.

4. Size does matter

Big school = more people, more majors, more money for chem-istry laboratories, and only sometimes a better football team. A large school may also mean lecture classes of hundreds, a lack of guidance from your advisors, or an administration that, instead of saying, "We can't help you, Joe," says, "We cannot aid you in your stated issues student #40522054." This is not universally true; many larger institutions have implemented a variety of innovative programs to ensure you get all the help and personal attention you need. Nor is it true that small colleges always have a small endowment or limited high-tech facilities or small classes where you will call your professors by their first names. These are mere stereotypes and while there may be a grain of truth in them, it is critical to find out more about how each individual college deals with the issues created by its size.

The one thing that numbers *will* tell you is how many students attend a school. But a big number of students doesn't equate to thousands of friends. If you go to a school of 40,000, it is far easier to fall off the face of the Earth and to go entire days without speaking to anyone than if you go to a school of 1,200 people. Very few people are actually this isolated, but at a big school you can easily walk into a lecture hall full of people and know no one. Small colleges are analogous (though not perfectly) to smaller towns. You walk into a party and realize you know seven people out of ten and you didn't know that all of them know each other, too. You sit down to dinner all by yourself, and in moments, vague acquaintances flock to join you. Your friend's cousin's roommate's friend from Spanish class broke up with your friend's other roommate's friend's sister and now they're not talking. Again this is by no means a universal—it is possible to be a recluse in any environment and possible you will not get to know (or like) people any easier in a smaller environment. But you should consider how things really are no matter where you go.

Again the trick is to know your own style and which type of environment suits you best.

This isn't your final decision folks, so relax . . . the real pressure won't be on quite yet. For now, just keep these things in

If you were afraid of not having time to meet all your neighbors, imagine living in a building with the population of a small town. The United States Naval Academy has the world's largest dormitory, housing over 4,000 midshipmen.

mind while daydreaming about the pictures on those pretty brochures. You just might want to visit some schools before applying to see if they're your style. If you have the time and money to visit some colleges before application time, go for it. For information on how to make the most of your college visits, see our section on "Visiting Colleges" in the Post-Acceptance Party chapter.

OK, Now Decide!

All of a sudden, you're a senior in high school and you'll need to decide where you want to spend all of your parents money . . . and the next four years of your life. You've probably narrowed it down a little by now—you know for sure that you're not attending Joe and Bob's College of Mixology . . . unless they give you a great package. So what to do next? The following is a cheat sheet for making a list of colleges to apply to, so use it in any way that suits you. After all, this book is about *how* to get in, not *where* (no matter how many jokes we might make about Yale).

Those application fees can really pile up, not to mention the fees for sending off financial aid reports to all prospective colleges, so you'll want to develop a list whose length is based on how much cash you're willing to shell out just to apply. Sit down with a list of all the schools you liked along the way (keeping in mind all the stuff we told you in the last section) and start really narrowing it down. That way you don't blow all the money you will need later for books.

With the help of your guidance counselor, or whatever mentor you've picked to do the job your counselor is seemingly paid not to do, you should pick between three and nine colleges to apply to, broken down into the following categories:

1-3 "reach" schools:
The likelihood of making it into these schools might be slim, but you have a shot and should always keep these dream colleges in mind. After all, you'll never get in if you don't apply.

1-3 "appropriate" schools:
You're not a shoe-in at these schools, but if you work your hardest and smile during the interview, these are the schools most likely to accept you and still challenge you once you're in.

1-3 "safety" schools:
In case that interview comes on a particularly bad day for you, and those pie-in-the-sky schools only send you form-letter rejections, you don't want to be left with nowhere to go. Select a

Ever wondered why the University of Vermont is called UVM instead of UVT, or even just UV? The letters UVM are based on a derivation of the school's Latin name, Universitas Viridis Montis, or the University of the Green Mountains.

few schools that you really should get into with your academic background and also ones that you would be happy attending if the luck of the admissions game weren't to go your way.

Sit down and plot all the important dates for application materials for every school on your list and make sure you have time to do it all without ruining your group science presentation (due on the fifteenth, no extensions!).

Call 'em up and request all necessary application materials. Do this as soon as possible to have time to fill out everything nice and neatly.

A Note for Parents

Let's face it, you were probably the one who decided that your kid needed this book anyhow. You care about your kids and want the best for them; this goes without saying. However, contrary to many of your "helping" impulses, the best thing you can do at this point (during the sophomore and junior year) is to avoid putting excessive pressure on your child. This does not mean completely bowing out of the application process. There is a useful role the conscientious parent can play.

Help with organization. Those letters and brochures will come flooding in, even for a C student; if you don't believe us now, you will. When they do, find that shoebox or file folder or paper bag and gently remind your special little guy or gal to keep the materials organized. If your child is interested in a specific college, help him or her to request additional information by letter, e-mail, or telephone.

Learn along with them. Maybe you bought one of those college guides that rates colleges—say four stars for academics or 87

If the rainy weather in your neck of the woods has got you down, maybe you could transfer to the College of the Desert in the Coachella Valley of California, where on average only three inches of rain falls a year.

Source:
www.caa-aqua.org

The California Institute of Technology boasts a faculty to student ratio of 1 to 3. If you don't think that makes a better college, you better take it up with *U.S. News and World Report*, who named CalTech the best college in the country in August 1999.

percent for admissions. Keep in mind that these ratings are nearly entirely subjective—don't panic if that top-choice school isn't among U.S. News and World Report's top 50—learn more about it. How is it unique? How hard is it to change majors? Read that mail even if your child doesn't. Surf the web with them or on your own. Learn as much as you can.

Talk to them about what they want. Without giving the old "what are you gonna do with your life" speech, sit down at some point and figure out what priorities your child has. You may discover your son is, unbeknownst to you, entertaining thoughts of becoming a doctor. Your daughter does not want to become merely an engineer, but an electrical engineer, and may explain at some length the difference between the two. Talk a little yourself, talk about your college experience if you think you can get away with it (we trust you know what not to tell them about college). Talk about what priorities you had and how well they worked, about your favorite classes and experiences, about things you never got the chance to do and wish you had. They're listening more than you know; make sure you're listening to them at least as much.

Make recommendations judiciously and with great restraint

Your kids inevitably fall into one of three categories. When you ask, "What about X University?" they will say:

A. "Yeah, OK, fine. That sounds good."

B. "Why do you always try to tell me what to do with my life? I wouldn't go there in a million years!"

C. Choice A on Monday, Wednesday, and alternate Fridays; B on Tuesdays and Thursdays.

You may not realize the extent to which you influence your child, who, at least at some level, wants to make you happy. He or she might acquiesce or protest violently, but regardless of the outward expression, pushing a particular school may force your child into believing there is no other choice. Your kid must be an active participant in the college-search process in order for all of you, as a group of collaborators, to come to a satisfying conclusion.

In the end, you should consider the following carefully: with the amount of money you'll be putting into this education, you have every right to guide your kids on their search, but you also don't want them to end up dropping out of *your* favorite univer-

If you're looking for that certain pep that only the National Grand Champions of Collegiate Cheerleading can inspire, look into North Carolina State University, where the "Wolfpack" pep is supreme.

sity. We all know someone who's here because their parents wanted a Harvard kid in the family, and trust us, they're not usually the happiest kid in the bunch. One junior at Harvard tells us "I wanted to go to culinary school so badly, but my parents made me apply to Harvard. Now they're going to have to pay for the three years I'm planning at Johnson and Wales. I hope they're ready to mortgage the house." Listen to their dreams and remember that the young have an uncanny ability to actually follow them.

CHAPTER FOUR

A Whole Other Ballgame

The College Search as an Athletic Recruit

If you're an athlete, your college search will likely be very different from the searches of your nonathletic peers. Instead of debating which frats are the coolest, you will spend your time debating which team is the coolest. Instead of taking weekend jaunts with parents to various schools, you will visit schools on all-expense-paid bashes called "recruiting" trips. Instead of praying that the admissions office likes the paper version of you, you will be dealing with real-life coaches and academic representatives both on the phone and in the flesh. Your decision deadlines will often differ from those of your friends, putting you on a completely different schedule, and instead of only weighing academics, you'll be weighing classes and athletics, while trying to measure the feasibility of both. You won't be bored.

Your application may also be given additional attention in the admissions office. Though procedure varies by school, most coaches are allowed a ballpark figure of athletes they can "slide in," i.e., get accepted. Usually, one or two will be slid past with minimal questions asked, and the rest will need to display academic standards appropriate to the school. Some schools are known for their many "athletic admissions," i.e. students accepted with lower academic standards; other schools are known for not allowing athletic admissions. Ask around, and pretty much anyone in the loop will be able to tell you which schools do what.

If a coach is allowed, say, around seven admissions each year, this means that the coach will be pushing athletes on whether or not the school in question is their first choice. If you say it is, the coach will hopefully consider you one of their seven. This said, don't lie, because you're robbing someone else of a slot. Also, coaches talk, and you don't want to start out on the wrong foot with your new coach.

Many coaches will advise wanted-but-not-prized athletes to apply early decision without putting their names on the Almighty List. If they're deferred, their names go back on the List. It's a good option, so consider taking it if offered.

To Be or Not to Be a Recruit

How do you know if you are one of the prized few? Answer: *You are a recruited athlete if a coach calls you more than once, offers you an official visit to the school, or visits you off campus.* Many coaches will spend the first contact or two just getting to know you, so don't stress if no large financial offers are made immediately. Not a big deal.

Once you are officially a recruit, what happens next varies by sport. In some sports, such as football and wrestling, prospective coaches need to watch you in action to see how good you are. This means that a coach might find out where you're competing and come watch. Many recruits don't know this, but if you would prefer to not know when your prospective coach will be observing you, tell them! Give them a bunch of competition dates, and they'll come down and introduce themselves to you afterward, saving you a lot of palm sweat.

In other less subjective sports, such as swimming and running, a time on a piece of paper and a phone call gives coaches the information they need. In these

In 1939, the University of Oregon won the first Men's Basketball NCAA tournament, beating Ohio State by a score of 46 to 33 before a near-capacity crowd of 5,500.

Source: www.ncaa.org

cases, your personality matters a bit more, as it's their main criteria for judging you, so be cool.

As a general rule, coaches are banned from contacting/stalking you via telephone until the July 1st after your junior year, though they are allowed to start assaulting your mailbox as early as September 1st of your junior year, and may approach your hometown coach. Many college coaches will have academic faculty and members of the team send you snail mail or email as well.

As another general rule, football is its own thing, with its own extremely complex and seemingly pointless rules. Early decision deadlines, letter of intent deadlines, and all that other jazz also vary vastly by sport, with football players truly jammin' to the beat of their own special drummer. To find out about all NCAA rules, we recommend getting a free copy of the "NCAA Guide for the College-Bound Student-Athlete," also available at www.ncca.com. The NCAA has turned itself into such a complicated organization that you'll need their guide to get through all their red tape.

I Wanna Be a Recruit but I'm Not

The number one way to ensure that you'll be recruited is to send letters profiling yourself to prospective college coaches in the spring of your junior year, particularly to your "reach" schools. Coaches are experts in coaching, not mind reading—without your help they'll have no idea that you're interested in their program. Pivotal information to mention in your letter includes your name, your contact information, your school, your SAT/ACT scores, an indication of your grades (honor list, high honors, etc.), some mention of any awards won, and an accurate assessment of your athletic skills. This is not the time to be modest. Also, it's a good idea to stick in some lines specific to the college at hand, such as "I am excited at the prospect of attending Bordine College, for both the opportunity of training in your program and the chance to study under your world-renowned Mythology department." Whatever you do, make sure to change the specific details for different colleges, because the Bodunk College coach will be less than pleased to hear about rival Bordine's Mythology program.

Oh, You're So Recruit Material

Just because you're not your school's MVP doesn't mean that you're not recruit material. Many students miss out on recruiting opportunities by not realizing that their athletic skills are marketable. During your junior spring, research various college athletic teams to find one that would fit your abilities, aiming for the top to middle of the program.

Top college secret: Often, high-quality academic schools have some not-so-strong athletic teams. This means that even with your medium-tier skills, you could be considered a valuable asset. These mediocre teams are the perfect loophole for you to get into and enjoy an awesome school, while playing the sport you love. Work the system.

The NCAA and Eligibility

You need to register with the NCAA to be eligible for recruitment. The NCAA is like any really large organization—they, too, can mess up paperwork, lose pivotal documentation, and drop digits off SAT scores, all of which would result in your being deemed ineligible. This said, register as early as possible with the NCAA if you think there's the slightest chance you may chat with a college coach. Then check and double check, and save all your paperwork, because it would be a real shame to find out you're ineligible after there's any time left to do something about it.

By the same token, do make sure that you actually are eligible for recruitment. Academic standards are minimal, based on proof of high school graduation, a minimal spread of curricula that

---

If you plan to play NCAA Division I basketball in college, try to have your team break the record for most consecutive victories. What is the record you ask? The UCLA Bruins won 88 consecutive games from 1971-1974.

Source:
www.factmonster.com

---

should be required for high school graduation, and a barely acceptable GPA + SAT/ACT index score. If you're worried, contact the NCAA. If your grades are higher than Cs and your combined SATs over 900, confine your worries to the NCAA paperwork department.

All Those Rules

Of course, in order to reap the wonderful benefits of athleticism, you need to be aware of the general procedure surrounding your sport's recruiting process. The NCAA rules surrounding high school recruitment are extremely strict.

Our advice: Don't break 'em.

Luckily, most rules come down on the side of coaches. General themes include not smothering prospective athletes, not stalking them, and not buying them cool stuff (sorry). This means that if your prospective coach offers you a new, fully loaded BMW with built-in massagers and a sunroof, you need to say no. But do compliment her on her good taste. It also means that if you feel the urge to offer a prospective coach a new, fully loaded BMW with built-in massagers and a sunroof, you need to refrain. (Though you, too, have good taste. And there's no rule against gifts to the authors of this book, in case you were wondering.)

If you plan on retaining your eligibility, think like the NCAA. Profess your identity as a wholesome student athlete participating in amateur athletics all for the fun of the game. Do not accept professional money of any kind or sign your life away to anything

If you plan to play NCAA Division I basketball, we hope you're used to having millions of people watch you play. In the 1979 Final Four game between Magic Johnson's Michigan State team and Larry Bird's Indiana State, 18 million viewers tuned in on their TVs.

Source:
www.infoplease.com

resembling an agent, advertising, or other compromising contract.

Important note: Giving lessons to neighborhood children is somehow considered by the NCAA as the acceptance of professional money. Many people break this rule, but they also keep it under the table. (Among other things, that means they don't list it as a form of employment on their college applications.) Our advice is to do your community some good and give those lessons for free. There are more lucrative ways to earn money without hurting your chances at college athletic participation.

All Those Divisions

Each Division—Division I, II, III, NAIA and NCCAA—has its own rules. Consult your handy-dandy "NCAA Guide for the College-Bound Student-Athlete," because a lot of them are baffling. The take-home message is that only Division I schools can offer you athletic scholarships. The other divisions and the Ivy League are forbidden from offering scholarship money other than financial aid. And they are banned from offering you extra amounts of financial aid in order to compensate for the athletic scholarships they can't give you—financial aid offices at these scholls treat both athletes and non-athletes with the same loving care.

Non-Monetary Perks

The main draw to non-scholarship athletic programs, besides the help they might lend in getting in, is that they offer you a great environment where everyone is participating in athletics for the love of the game, as opposed to love of the scholarship. Many non-scholarship

Schools are not allowed to pay for your official recruiting visit until you've shown them your PSAT, SAT, ACT, or PLAN score.

Source: The NCAA Division I Manual, 2001–2002.

If you're not a student-athlete, don't look down on jocks. After all, in 1993, 58 percent of collegiate athletes graduated, compared to 56 percent of the whole student body.

Source: NCAA Graduation Rate Report, 2000.

schools have quite vigorous athletic programs that regularly produce top athletes—particularly Ivy League schools—so don't feel like you will commit athletic suicide by going to a non-scholarship school.

Regardless of scholarship status, athletes usually enjoy other non-monetary bonuses such as special athlete dorms and dining halls, which offer more conveniently located living facilities and athletically oriented food. (Read: All you can eat, all the time. Yay!)

Some schools offer academic perks. For example, Cal Berkeley athletes get first dibs on classes due to their practice schedules. We've heard of Cal students taking over four years to graduate due to difficulty getting into required courses. This means that not only can Cal athletes create for themselves awesome schedules, such as the infamous

"Monday/Wednesday/Friday/Saturday/Sunday Vacation Schedule," they can also guarantee entrance into required classes.

Whatever you do, *make sure* you'd still want to attend your college without these perks, in case you decide to quit athletics. We know it seems impossible now, but it has been known to happen.

Pros and Cons of Athletic Scholarships

The pros of athletic scholarships are clear: A paid-for education and happy parents. This said, we're going to focus on the cons. Though these cases are the exception rather than the rule, once you accept an athletic scholarship, you are essentially a paid employee, albeit a very well-paid employee. Your coach is basically your employer. While most college athletes like their coaches and build wonderful relationships that continue long after college, if you don't like something about your training program or the lack of time to spend in other college activities, there's very little you can do about it if your coach disagrees.

Most scholarship athletes participate in very few other activities. The worst possible situation for a college athlete is to realize after a year that they hate their college lifestyle, but feel binded into it by their family's financial need. (Transferring is always an option, but never an easy one.) This said, *make sure* you like your team and coach, because you're going to be spending lots of time with them.

If a college recruiting officer contacts you before July 1st after your junior year in high school, you might find it interesting to know that according to the NCAA bylaws (for many sports) it is against the rules for him to do that.

Source: The NCAA Division I Manual, 2001–2002.

Ugly situations have been known to arise when colleges hire new coaches midway through your collegiate career. There's very little you can do about this phenomenon besides being aware of the possibility, so keep your ear to the ground within your athletic department.

Another pivotal tidbit: Scholarships are *not* guaranteed for four years and have to be renewed each year. This means that if you fall, break your leg, and can never compete again, your scholarship could be revoked. It also means that if you decide that collegiate athletics aren't for you, your education is no longer paid for. Ask your prospective coach what will happen if you hit a lull. Many coaches will guarantee a four-year ride, regardless of the circumstances, but check with other students and coaches about this coach's reliability to make sure he can be trusted—you don't want to be forced out of a school you love when your scholarship gets pulled.

We can't emphasize enough the importance of making sure you like other aspects of your school besides the sports team, because if you tear your ACL while playing a drunken capture-the-flag game with your team and can no longer compete, you're still at that school.

Athletics or Academics?

Though the NCAA strives to create "student-athletes," meatheads are still an abundant variety in the wide world of collegiate athletics. To make sure that your program will value education, check the GPAs and graduation rates for your sport. Ask team members how they juggle athletics and academics, and make sure your priorities generally match

If you are visiting a college that is trying to recruit you and staying with a student-athlete, the school is allowed to give him or her $30 to entertain you, a free meal, and free admission to a sporting event. Make them spend that $30 on something cool, like some awesome CDs.

Source: The NCAA Division I Manual, 2001–2002.

A college woman's golf coach can give a prospect private lessons, but only if he or she also makes lessons available to the public.

Source: The NCAA Division I Manual, 2001–2002.

the trend of your team. Also, make sure that professors look at athletes favorably because you will definitely be missing classes for competitions. There's nothing worse than a jock-hating professor or teaching assistant. They can and will fail you. Upperclassmen will know all about these, as well as how to avoid them, but it will be hard if this variety makes up the entire faculty. (Extreme dorks who were taunted by jocks as children can hold lifelong grudges, and they're now in a position of power over you.) You want an athletic-friendly school.

First Contact: The Coach Quandary

When talking to prospective coaches, be both yourself and somewhat honest. Many coaches pick athletes partially on personality, so be fun! Phone conversations should be enjoyable!

Dishonesty about your plans is considered rude and poor form—just like you're shopping for colleges, they're shopping for athletes, and they won't appreciate your leaving them hanging. Coaches usually compete for athletes with similar schools and often know other coaches personally, so keep your story straight. In the case of scholarship athletes, another student's offer depends on what you do, so take your time, but let a coach know as honestly as possible when you've decided to not attend their school.

If you can't decide which school to attend, it is all right to pretend to not be home when coaches call. Instead, warn family members if you're expecting a call and don't pick up the phone.

Sample phone call:

"Hello?"

"Hello Mrs. Adams, this is Dick Jamison from Broonke College. Is Sarah available?"

[repeating to Sarah, pretending to write it down] "Dick Jamison from Broonke . . . . I'm not sure she's here right now."

[Sarah nods vigorously to her mother and loudly shuts a door for a masterful "I've just come in" effect.]

"Oh wait, she's just come in. Sarah, it's Dick Jamison from Broonke College."

For football recruits, institutional staff members of recruiting colleges are not allowed to watch you play to evaluate your athletic ability more than three times during an academic year. However, if they evaluate you more than one time during a day, that counts as one time.

Source: The NCAA Division I Manual, 2001–2002.

This routine allows you to decide who you want to talk to and comes highly recommended.

Coaches are required to give you specified quiet/dead periods during which contact is forbidden. The idea is that you'll have time to think to yourself. Take advantage of this time.

The Recruiting Trip

Coaches who are truly interested in your attending their school will often offer you a recruiting trip. (Whether or not they offer is generally a good indication of how much they want you, though schools with small budgets may not be able to offer you a visit.) On a so-called "Official Visit," your travel and meal expenses are covered, though there is a reasonable daily limit to how much they can spend on you (sorry). Your trip is limited to 48 hours on campus, and you will be housed with current team members.

The general idea is for you to experience a few days at the college. These few days can also be quite fun, as students aim to show you a good time. This is *not* the time to experiment with extreme college drinking. The alcohol will still be there when you return as a student in five months, though the amount of alcohol and drunkenness you see is a good indication of how the average student-athlete at that school spends his or her social time. Keep in mind that coaches often bring students in on fun weekends, such as during campus-wide festivals, and that the college may not be like that normally.

Feel free to ask team members as many questions as you'd like, though it's generally recommended that recruits be somewhat quiet and subservient on

College recruiters would get in big trouble if they were caught offering you any of these things: clothes or equipment, free housing, giving a job or a loan to a relative of yours, use of athletic facilities, or sponsorship for a sports awards banquet.

Source: The NCAA Division I Manual, 2001–2002.

new territory. Peppiness and enthusiasm are fine, but know your place—just like you're checking them out, they're checking you out. Talk to roommates, ask about academics and after-hours socializing. Make sure to subtly ask a team member whether an athlete of your ability would compete on their team or not—some coaches will promise recruits play time, only to have those recruits spend four years on a junior varsity team or on the bench—as well as how athletes tend to perform senior year as compared to freshman year. Otherwise, just kick back and have a good time while being as observant as possible. Many recruits have a "yes, I want to go here" feeling that defies explanation, so you may just know. Otherwise, keep lookin'.

The Money

So you've decided to take the plunge and accept a scholarship. How the money works:

Each sport has a limited budget for scholarships, some of which is tied up in current athletes. This means that if your prospective school admitted an unusually large freshman class last year in your sport, that's not a good thing for you because that class is most likely commanding a large chunk of scholarship funds. By the same token, a school that will be graduating a number of seniors when you graduate from high school will be freeing up some scholarship funds, some of which could have your name on it.

Your recruitment also depends on the abilities of your recruiting class—i.e. if three of the best athletes in the world in your specialty are all graduating American high schools your year, you may not have a chance at the top scholarships (most schools only recruit one or two athletes for each specialty). This said, research the current team to see its specialties and keep a general eye on other recruits. When in doubt, ask a prospective coach, and they might answer somewhat truthfully. (They may also lie.) These factors are out of your control, but it is up to you to know where you stand and manipulate that position to the best of your ability.

Though the financial aid office is not allowed to offer you any special grants because of your athletic status, scholarship students can still receive financial aid from schools, though scholarship money will be taken into account. Many coaches use this loophole to their advantage, giving students "combination" scholarships, i.e. a mishmash of

If you really want to play NCAA golf, don't make the same mistake University of Alabama sophomore Jason Bohn did when he entered a charity hole-in-one championship and won a million dollars, which rendered him ineligible under NCAA rules.

Source:
www.colleges.com

athletic scholarship and financial aid funding. This solution allows your education to be well-funded, while leaving a greater portion of scholarship funding in a coach's budget. There are lots of rules about this on the coach's side of things, but, if you think it's a possibility, ask.

Once you are a student, coaches can offer you no special benefits. (You won't find your coach letting you make long-distance calls from the office phone.) You also won't be allowed to make any money off your athletic ability, whether in the form of professional advertisements or teaching lessons to kids, though many do the latter under the table. These restrictions exist to prevent you from receiving the benefits of former generations, particularly poorer athletes who ended up with a free Mercedes, jewelry, and airfare to non-athletic Caribbean venues, all under the guise of an athletic system budget. Your generation is left with only the vague special treatment of first dibs on classes, special athlete facilities, and all the notoriety and social status of jockdom. Good luck.

CHAPTER FIVE

The Application

In order to give you a better sense of how to go about filling out the actual application, we have gone through and analyzed—sometimes in minute and excruciating detail—each section of the average (dare we say, common?) application. To those who might find this unnecessary, more power to you. But to those who picked up the book and immediately flipped to this section, take comfort in the fact that you are not alone—those fill-in-the-blanks never seemed so intimidating. What might seem at first glance like the easy part of the application becomes scarier when you realize that it's the first representation of you that your top-choice school will see. It is sometimes the most seemingly unimportant details (the blue vs. black ink phenomenon) that bring about the most stress. So, diligent applicant, rather than bug your college counselor for the umpteenth time over which activities look best or what ethnic group to check, just flip to the relevant heading for our own analysis.

Personal Data

This section is definitely the most straightforward part of the application. If you are applying to college, you'd better be competent enough by now to fill out your legal name and permanent home address. A message from the wise: If your friends affectionately call you "Stoner," "Spanks," or "Chick-a-day Ray" you might want to refrain from listing it as your preferred name. As far as the address category goes, if you attend a boarding school, you should list your school address as your mailing address in order to receive correspondence from the school in a timely manner.

The only somewhat stressful parts of this section are the questions pertaining to academic interests, possible field career plans, and special college or division. Don't spend too much time pondering all the different interpretations of what you put ("If I say I want to study drama, are they going to think I'm not serious about my academics?" or "If I put 'politics' as my career plan are they going to think I'm too schmoozy?"). The only reason this is here is to give schools a better concept of your potential field of study; what you list is only a means of better classifying you and has little influence on your application status.

Perhaps the most controversial aspect of the application is the optional section pertaining to ethnicity, birthplace, and language. When they say optional, they certainly mean optional. You should not feel pressured to list anything or to fit yourself into any of the categories. The list of choices has become more detailed and extensive over the last few years and now incorporates the specific countries of origin rather than just regions, an acknowledgement that, though both are considered Asian, being Korean and being Cambodian are very different from one another. If you come from a mixed-ethnic background, check away—they asked for it. You know you've always wanted the opportunity to share that you are one-quarter Navajo, one-quarter Pacific Islander, one-quarter Panamanian and one-quarter Lebanese. Also, feel free to make use of the "other" category. If you identify strongly with your local Greek community, then listing "Greek" is appropriate. On the other hand, if your family has lived in Central Michigan since the pioneer days, checking the "White/Caucasian" box is probably most accurate and shouldn't damage your ethnicity self-esteem. If you have the opportunity to (truthfully) check a box that designates you as a minority, you should check away. Many schools, although they might not outright say it, use this information to ensure that each class is racially and ethnically more balanced. In other words, it can only help you. So don't feel like you're abusing your heritage to get into school, you're just helping them get a picture of the mix for each class.

Educational Data

Pretty basic, really. List all schools you've attended, as well as colleges you've taken classes at during high school. If your family has moved around a lot, just attach a separate sheet of paper with all the schools you attended during high school, even if some were for only a few months. Also, if you've attended any summer programs for credit, make sure to list those, too. It looks impressive if you've spent your non-school time doing schoolwork.

Perhaps the most important aspect of this section only pertains to students who know they are taking time off between high school and college. These applicants are asked to write a brief statement discussing what they are doing in their time away from school. This should be a little reminder to all of you taking time off that you will want to have something productive to insert here. Unfortunately, "sitting on my duff and watching digital cable" does not count as productive. How much better do "volunteering for my local congressional campaign," "building sewer systems in Myanmar," "working at Burger King to save for college," or simply "taking care of my grandparents" sound? Even if you are just taking the year to chill out and de-stress or reapply to colleges, you might want to try and pad your application with some additional activities or work experience.

Test Information

While the application has two blanks for SAT and ACT testing dates, over-zealous students and poor test-takers alike choose to take the tests more than that. If you are one of those, remember to list your two *best* scores. The same goes for the SAT II tests—there are six spaces, though you are only required to take three tests. If you have taken more and are proud of your scores, definitely list them. Just remember that the schools will get your official results from the ETS, so no fiddling with numbers—nothing looks more fishy to an admissions officer than someone who has taken the opportunity to blatantly lie on their application.

Family

For many, this section seems somewhat misplaced in the application. What does it matter if your parents are married or not and
where your siblings go to school? Well, the reason they ask these
questions is mainly to get a better concept of the context in which
you grew up. For example, if your parents got divorced during the
spring of your sophomore year, it might help the admissions
officer account for the sudden drop in your grades. Furthermore,
looking at your family background helps to contextualize you a
bit. It looks quite impressive if neither of your parents nor any
siblings attended college and you are a straight-A student with
top SAT scores. On the flip side, if your parents are obviously
well-educated or wealthy, there might be less tolerance for a
spotty academic record or lackluster school participation. It
might be held against you if you have not taken full advantage of
the privileges you happened to have been born with.

If one or both of your parents are graduates from one of the
places you are applying to, it will be noted that you are a "legacy,"
which can hold anything from a minimal to a considerable
amount of weight, depending on the college and on the relationship your parents have with their alma mater. At the many private
universities that depend on fund-raising to operate, kids of
alumni who have a history of generous contributions may be
favored to keep the money rolling in.

As far as your parents' occupations go, the application states
"describe briefly" to avoid the simple listing of "businessman" or

"receptionist." Instead try listing "Director of Northeast Regional Sales, Peptic" or "Receptionist, Fido's Food Factory." Alternatively, if your mother is a lawyer, you probably don't need to list that she specializes in tax law.

All this said, the "Family" section, barring a few pretentious schools that really love lineage (and their money), will never be the make-or-break part of your application. So don't stress this one too much—just fill it out and move right along to the next section.

Academic Honors

The verdict is in. This part of the application was designed solely to make you stretch the truth and brag about yourself. Be consoled by the fact that thousands of high school applicants across the country will be doing the same. So take a deep breath and resign

yourself to something you should learn at this stage of life: You can stretch things a little to make them sound somewhat more impressive than they were originally—as long as you don't blatantly lie—in order to make yourself look better to strangers. So that third-place prize you won in a Spanish poetry recitation contest should be included. And yes, you can turn that certificate that everyone who participated in the Math Team receives into a "Math Team Award." Don't be modest on this section.

If you're an amazing overachiever and have so many academic honors that the few blank spaces that they give you just won't cut it, you have the advantage of picking the few most important honors that you would like to list. The best advice we can give you on what to list is as follows. Be sure to include any honors that are *really* amazing, like

---

Here are a few extracurricular activities you may want to leave off your application:

- Studying

- Volunteer Hall Monitor

- Detention and/or Suspension

- Water boy for the JV Tetherball (or Golf) Team

"Intel Prize Winner," or "State AP scholar." Next, list the honors that meant the most to you to win. Stuff like character awards or writer's prizes are pretty common, but if they mean a whole lot to you, the admissions committee will see that by their inclusion here, and it will help them to draw up their initial picture of you as a student. Whatever you do, don't write in extra-tiny print to fit in every honor that you've received, even if they're all impressive. If you really feel like more needs to be said about your academic awards and honors, it's best to list in the blanks the stuff that's the biggest or most important to you and then refer application readers to an included resume. This is helpful because it lets the reader of your application have the option of going through every honor or just glimpsing them over. They won't find it presumptuous to send a resume, either: they know those blanks get stuffed quickly and that you might want to tell them more when they're considering everything more closely, but they need to go through so many applications through the year that they really only want the basics about you right there on the app.

Extracurricular, Personal, and Volunteer Activities

So, you arrive at the "activities" section and you either:

A. Couldn't be more pumped to fill this puppy out. Here is where the last four years of martyring yourself for the sake of everything under the after-school sun pays off. Thank God you're allowed to attach a separate sheet—there is *no* way all of your accomplishments could fit on one page.

B. Panic. Oh my God, why do they give you seven lines? Do they expect you to have that much to put down? Wait; define "activity." Does hanging out at the mall or watching TRL religiously on MTV count? You did join the Carson Daly fan club—that counts as an activity, right?

C. Start filling it out—it's just another step in the application process. You dedicated yourself mostly just to soccer and choir, but have one or two other things from freshman and sophomore year you could throw in to fill up a few more lines.

If you answered "C," you'll find yourself in a category with many other college applicants. There are the Activity-Obsessed, the Activity-Less, and then there's you. You've focused on a

Don't feel too bad if your application doesn't look too good, since colleges themselves send out documents with mistakes to students. For example, one all-women's college has sent out a mailing addressed to "prestigious young women," and on the information request card has you check off your sex.

Source: "Come to my kollege" by Brittany Griffin in U. Magazine. Cited online at www.colleges.com

few things, but haven't spread yourself too thin. What this illus-trates is both your level of commitment and your good judgment, two qualities which admissions officers are looking for.

Thankfully, there are very few who would answer "A," but for those who meet the description, congratulations. Admissions officers across the country will recognize your hard work and commitment. That said, there has been a growing consensus in admissions literature lately warning students away from listing too many activities. Your best bet might be to put down your top seven activities and leave off some of the more random ones you only did for a few months freshman or sophomore year. What you are trying to illustrate is your responsibility and allegiance. Officers would rather see that you've focused yourself on a few things that truly interested you rather than dabbling in many, as we've mentioned in a previous chapter.

Clearly, this dilemma of what to list and what to omit is not an issue for those who answered "B." If that description best matches your activity track record, there's not much you can do about it at this point—hopefully your grades and SAT scores will make up for your lack of writing under this category.

One more thing . . . For those of you stretching your extracur-riculars for all they're worth, keep in mind that nifty little column with the heading "hours per week." Just in case you forgot, there are only 24 hours in a day and 168 hours in a week. Keep in mind that most high school students spend about seven hours in class each week day, sleep an average of seven hours a night, have about two hours of homework on week nights, and allocate about an hour three times a day for meals. Input all those numbers into that nifty activity calculator and voila: there are only about 53 or so free hours during the week in which you could possibly take part in any activities—and that's counting weekends. So make sure it all adds up before you have to explain to your interviewer your ability to stay awake for six days on end and still manipulate space and time to fit in badminton practice.

Work Experience

The definition of "work experience" is something many applicants grapple with. What actually counts as a job? Do you have to get paid? Do internships count? What about babysitting? A lemonade stand? The section is intentionally vague on this definition, allowing for some much-appreciated room for interpreta-

The common application is a common site for admissions officers in 227 colleges. About half of them require a supplement, however.

To download the common application from the commonapp.org web site, you have to have at least 4 MB of RAM and 2 MB of hard disk space free.

Source:
www.commonapp.org

tion. For the purpose of the application, work should count as any job you held in which you were hired and employed, regardless of whether or not you were paid. If you have been so innovative as to start your own company—whether it be a website, a lawn-mowing service, or a jewelry-making business—definitely milk that for all it's worth. What your work experience tells admissions officers is two-fold. First, it can serve to illustrate your commitment to a particular activity or interest. If you are editor of the school newspaper and think you might want to go into journalism, then a summer internship at a local magazine nicely complements your spinning of yourself as a journalist. Alternatively, an after-school job at Dunkin' Donuts helps to depict a more practical side. It shows that you are able to combine school and work, if need be. This can also explain why maybe your list of activities is not as extensive as you would have liked. Admissions offices realize and respect the fact that some applicants may have had to sacrifice playing in the band or on the field hockey team for financial reasons.

In terms of filling out the specifics of the work chart, you probably want to err on the generous side for number of hours worked. If your summer job was supposed to be 9 A.M. to 5 P.M., five days a week, but your boss usually let you out around 3 P.M., you're pretty safe saying you worked a forty-hour week. As with activities, just keep in mind how many hours is too many—there is no way you can spend twenty hours a week working and another thirty participating in activities. You're not a robot, you're a normal high school student.

Letters of Recommendation

Let's face it, letters of recommendation can make or break your application. If your recommenders rave about you, it could push you in. If they are weak, it could mean that someone else gets that spot over you. Something to keep in mind is that this person is sort of a character witness. You're on trial and you have to pick two people to represent you. No pressure, really.

Choosing an Academic Recommender

When deciding on academic recommenders, try to find two people who will offer a diverse perspective. If your best subjects are history and English, it would be good to have one recommender who can comment on your superior work in math or science. This is particularly important, for example, if you have not-so-great grades in math and a teacher can write on how much effort you put into your studies, despite your problems with the material, or the progress you made over the course of the year. These are the types of things colleges want to hear. If this is not possible, don't push it; it is better to have two good recommendations in similar subjects than one glowing and one mediocre recommendation in diverse fields.

This should not suggest, however, that recommendations are solely meant to be character evaluations. The best recommendations prove that you are up to the academic challenge of the college you are applying to. If your grades on a subject are relatively low, good letters emphasize the difficulty of the grading stan-

People have used neat handwriting for centuries before college applications were invented. In fact, the art of calligraphy dates back to 3500 B.C. in Ancient Egypt.

dards and the progress you have shown in class. If your grades are high, these letters show that your marks are merited, not inflated, and that you are a serious learner rather than merely a grade-grubber. Admissions officers really depend on teacher evaluations when interpreting the meaning of your grades and listed accomplishments, so don't choose a recommender who only knows you as "a nice, diligent student." Unfortunately, nice guys don't always finish first in this process, whereas truly competent and passionate students usually do. It is essential to choose someone who can portray you as such.

One question that often comes up pertains to the year in which you worked with the recommender. Generally, it is best to have a teacher from your junior or senior year of high school. Admissions offices are going to be a little wary of someone whose letters—no matter how good they are—come from freshman and sophomore year teachers. That said, if a teacher you had a year or two back is eager to write on your behalf, especially if they want to say something like Susie was the best student I ever had in my thirty years of teaching, it would be crazy to pass that up. If you do decide to go with one teacher you haven't had for a few years, make sure that the other teacher is one you had more recently.

Supplemental Recommendations

If you do choose to include a supplemental recommendation, try to pick someone who can illuminate a side of you that you feel was not sufficiently covered by your application. What this means is that if you have one glowing recommendation from a science teacher, it is not necessary to have another recommendation from the scientist you worked for over the summer. The only situation in which you might consider this is if you truly feel that the science teacher offers a limited perspective on your abilities. Instead, your supplemental recommender might be a hockey coach—even if it is junior varsity—who can talk about your dedication and leadership on the team. Or, if one of your most significant accomplishments outside the classroom is being editor of the school newspaper, then it might be nice to have a letter from the advisor of the paper talking about your success as a team player, managing your peers, your organizational qualities, and innovative ideas. These are accomplishments that are often hard for teachers to

That white-out you're covering your application in was invented by the mother of Mike Nesmith of the rock band "The Monkees."

judge in an academic setting, hence the need for supplemental recommendations.

Something else to keep in mind is that, in this case, more is not better. Admissions officers look at so much material and so many students that they do not have time to read every story you wrote for the literary magazine or memorize every photo you took for the yearbook. One recital tape is impressive (if it is quality), but more than that can be downright annoying (particularly if they are mediocre). Rather than send a tape of every concert you've played in the last few years, you'd be better off putting together a "Best of Me" collection. If Destiny's Child can do it, you can, too.

The same theory goes for supplemental recommendations—two is usually enough. Do not ask each of your bosses at your last four summer jobs for letters; instead, pick the most recent or one at which you feel you most excelled. Along those same lines, if your soccer coach is writing you a letter then it is not necessary to have your assistant coach and development camp coach write you letters as well. Instead, opt for a supplemental letter from the student council advisor attesting to your success as class vice-president; these letters should highlight your different strengths as an applicant, not reinforce the same one over and over. And no matter who your recommender is, make sure he or she actually knows you and is willing to write a lengthy letter filled with personal details on your behalf. "From her transcript, this student seems like a dedicated student" is not the most impressive sentiment in a letter of recommendation. Your aunt may live next door to a former member of the Board of Trustees for Yale Medical School, but just because you had dinner with him once doesn't mean his three-line letter on your behalf is going to get you into Yale. (But it is Yale, so you never know.)

Thank You, Sir, May I Have Another?

Asking for a Recommendation

Asking for a recommendation can be a daunting experience, and rightfully so. Be nice, be humble, and don't be demanding. Keep in mind that your teacher is doing you a huge favor—she is by no means obligated to write on your behalf. Letters of recommendation can be anywhere from one to several pages, depending on the depth of the person's experience working with you. Remember that writing a recommendation is a process; no matter how long

Applying to UCLA? This year, UCLA received more than 41,500 freshman applications for a class of 4,200 new freshmen, an unprecedented number and one of the largest college application pools in history. Good luck!

the letter is, it will probably take some time to compose.

It is important to give your recommenders all pertinent materials—you want to make the process as easy for them as possible. Definitely include addressed and stamped envelopes with your letters. It might also help to include your list of activities, application essay, and one or two papers or tests from their class (complete with comments and grades) to remind teachers of the quality of the work you did in the class. You might consider including copies of all this material in folders to ensure that teachers keep all the information together.

If you are unsure if someone can write you a good recommendation, he or she is probably not the best person to ask. It's to your benefit to be up front with the person you are asking for the recommendation from. You might even say point-blank, "Would you be willing to write me a favorable recommendation?" If there is any hesitation on his or her part, we would strongly advise you look for someone else.

Often times, very popular teachers are flooded with college recommendation requests. Unless you believe that you are one of their top students or that you know the teacher very well, it might be better to look for another teacher. It does not help your application if your recommender sends out several letters for different applicants to the same school that all say basically the same thing. Believe it or not, this often happens, and it does not look good. Sometimes less popular or new teachers might be more flattered, have more time, and be more eager to write a letter for you. If you are coming from a school where many students are applying to the same colleges, again, keep in mind that the same admissions officers are going to be reading all the applications for your school. Pick a teacher who you feel will make you stand out in the eyes of the admissions committee.

Time Frame

Keep in mind the following time frame when asking teachers for recommendations.

Junior Year

SPRING TERM: Begin thinking of possible recommenders. When picking your classes for the following fall, perhaps try to get a teacher who you have had before and are considering asking to write you a letter.

Senior Year

SEPTEMBER: Early Action/Early Decision/Rolling Admissions candidates should begin talking to possible recommenders.

EARLY OCTOBER: Early Action/Early Decision/Rolling Admissions candidates should have asked and gotten materials to recommenders; Regular Decision candidates should begin talking to teachers.

EARLY NOVEMBER: Regular Decision candidates should get all their pertinent application materials to recommenders.

Personal Statement

For a detailed analysis of the personal statement see our chapter on the essay.

CHAPTER SIX

Our Chapter on the Essay

10,000 Words on Your 500

In 500 words or less, you are about to fit a true snapshot of yourself into the one part of your application that requires true thought: the essay. (Choosing between blue and black ink doesn't count as "true thought" even if it took you half an hour.)

Those 500 words are valuable, to you and to the admissions committee. To them, it can make or break a borderline application by exposing the applicant more deeply than will his score on the SATs. For you, this is your shot at showing those grizzled folks down in the admissions office who you really are, or at explaining away some of the shadier areas of your application. If you've been concentrating on spinning all those high numbers and great grades into a particularly interesting direction, here's your chance to clinch it. Or, if you feel like you've taken care of selling yourself, it's a great chance to talk about some other interesting aspect of yourself.

Regardless, we'll provide you with some thoughts on how to bare your soul in a way that just might be fresh and exciting to people who've already seen it all. Add a dash of editing advice, a couple of real essays, and you've got everything you need to make a fantastic banana split—or a very slick essay.

The Essay: Why They Like It and Why You Should, Too

So if it's not pure sadism, why do colleges throw admissions essays your way?

For starters it's one more way of getting information about you that doesn't involve numbers. The essay provides a glimpse of your personality that doesn't show up in the letter of recommendation your math teacher wrote (about your skill with polynomials) or in the report the alumni interviewer (who had trouble remembering your name) mailed in.

And personality does count. Part of the rich, varied experience of college is meeting a variety of people. Ergo, they're not going to admit only applicants who write, "I'm an introvert who likes to play computer games on Saturday night, while locked in my room." Equally disastrous would be a school made up solely of beauty queens, drum majors, or Olympic pentathletes. Admissions officers are looking for a little bit of everything.

Which means they are looking for nothing specifically. Sure, they'd like to see evidence of responsibility, loyalty, curiosity, individuality, and a real passion for learning in an essay—illustrating one of these or a similar trait is your ticket to success—but the single thing that the folks down in admissions hate is an essay that looks like it's been written to please them. One that's saccharine. Uninspired. Boring. Pretentious.

Imagine reading a couple dozen essays a day that go, "I have expressed my considerable interest in science through various outlets, including the chemistry and science clubs, and hope to expand this interest in college both through the extracurricular and academic opportunities provided." All other things being equal, if you're deciding who to advocate for the last spot in the class, are you more likely to stand up for a student who fills a page-and-a-half with rambling drivel or one who tells a story about a chemistry experiment gone awry? Or about the research she's done on elm trees? Or about how he always comes up with these weird theories explaining why people watch television.

Whether it's fair or not for the essay to figure heavily in the personality equation, you are hopefully by now an experienced writer of English and there's no reason you can't use the essay to your advantage.

What can you do with it? Use it to express yourself. Any good admissions essay requires certain elements: depth and specificity, clarity of self-expression, and true passion and interest in the subject you choose to address. Fortunately, beyond this, you can do almost anything. Somebody's tried just about every trick in the book, so before you think that you'll be writing the only poem or the only dramatic monologue or the one application using only four-letter words, think again. However, if this is something you can do well (find a brutally honest friend who agrees you do it well) then there's no reason not to go for it.

If you were *actually* stranded on a desert island without hope of rescue, one good person to have with you might be Richard Hatch, winner of the CBS game show *Survivor 1*.

The object of the essay is to write about yourself, to illustrate who you are. If you can do this best through a poem or by writing about someone else, then that's the best strategy. It can be risky. If you get carried away with your essay praising your grandpa or about your stuffed clown, Lulu, you haven't done your job—there's not a whole heckuva lot about *you* in there. The same problem can crop up in a story about your game-winning wicket at the state cricket tourney or about saving somebody's life in a car crash: any of these could be compelling reading, but if they don't reveal anything about you, then none of them do any good. It doesn't have to be shameless self-promotion; an excellent essay can be modest and still scream how great its writer is, even if that's never explicitly stated.

The key here is illustration. You need an essay that shows, rather than tells. Use stories, anecdotes and examples—anything—wherever possible to show exactly what you mean. Don't stop there, either. A bit of analysis, a few words on why that experience you wrote about mattered to you or whether or not you agree with grandpa's outlook on life can be crucial. You don't need to be blatantly obvious and there doesn't have to be a moral, in fact doing that badly could ruin a perfectly good essay ("and I learned if you try hard enough, you can always accomplish your dreams"). Just be sure to include a little something on why you're so passionate about whatever your topic is.

Your Mission: to get the person reading your essay to see how smart, funny, introspective, dauntless, courageous, wacky, driven, or caring you really are. You want to make yourself memorable. The following describes how you do it.

"Don't worry if you think your college essay sounds a little cheesy—almost no one I know doesn't cringe rereading theirs now."

—Junior, Wellesley College

Choose Your Own Adventure: Picking a Topic

Picking the right question to answer is half the battle. Fortunately, it's also the easy half: you'll write best about what interests you. A fun essay for you equals a fun essay for the guy who has to read it, which equals bonus points.

Those crazy people down in admissions have helped out by thoughtfully providing one or more questions to choose from. Exhibit 1 is an uninspired question from the common application:

> Describe a character in fiction, an historical figure, or a creative work (as in art, music, science, etc.) that has had an influence on you and explain that influence.

Compare this with one asked by the University of Chicago (widely known for its unnervingly energetic questions):

> At a crucial point in his career, the writer James Baldwin withdrew to a secluded spot in the Swiss Alps. "There," he later wrote, "in that absolutely alabaster landscape, armed with two Bessie Smith records and a typewriter, I began to try to recreate the life that I had first known as a child and from which I had spent so many years in flight . . . It was Bessie Smith, through her tone and her cadence, who helped me to dig back to the way I myself must have spoken . . . and to remember the things I had heard and seen and felt."

> Inevitably, certain things—recordings, household objects, familiar smells—help us to "dig our way back" to our past. Write about something that has enabled you to return to a forgotten part of your past.

Wow. At first blush, the stylistic gulf between these two questions seems vast, but they're really after very similar things: writing about something that is important to you, be it book or object. In fact, with minor changes, the same essay could be submitted to both colleges.

Colleges, even when they give you a choice of questions, don't vary much from a range of basic topics.

Common Essay Topics
Most significant extracurricular activity and its impact on your life.
Person or event that has influenced you.
Local, national, or international issue of importance to you.
Greatest challenge you've faced.
Favorite teacher or class and why you enjoyed him/her/it.
Work of fiction or art that you find moving and why.
Academic area of interest and why you find it interesting.
Why you are interested in the college you are applying to.
An instance when two sets of values important to you came into conflict and how you resolved said conflict.

Which one is the right topic for you? We've used the word passion quite a few times and without exception college admissions counselors are looking for passionate essays. Passion need not be an irrational, torrid love for a subject, conjuring up images of you laying big, slobbery kisses all over your biology textbook. In fact, it probably shouldn't. Passion means an honest and genuine interest or love for your topic, be it tennis, your job at the laun-dromat, or the Ebola virus. Again, this doesn't require a sappy love-fest in which you go to the thesaurus a few dozen times to find synonyms for "good." Instead you'll want to concentrate on showing that you've studied a topic enough to have thorough knowledge of it and pepper the essay with interesting and rele-vant details and anecdotes.

Pick a topic you love and most of all pick one you're comfort-able writing about—the only bad topics are the ones you write a boring or trite essay on. This said, there are a few no-no's for admissions essays—writing about stuff that makes you sound psycho, for instance. An essay on your successful career as a shoplifter or on your plan to kidnap the kid who lives across the street is obviously unacceptable. This is an admissions essay, not a full confession—leave criminal activity out.

Muddier territory includes subjects such as attempting sui-cide, eating disorders, and sexual experiences. The short answer is that these topics do not portray you in the strongest light possi-ble, so you ought to avoid them. Furthermore, if you are not fully comfortable with the topic, odds are neither will the admissions officer. Challenging your reader by making yourself out to be a complex person is wonderful. Freaking them out or even making them wonder if you'll survive your first year is not.

Naturally, there's another side to this. The essay is your chance to explore and expose yourself as completely as possible and if you've had to face difficult issues, they are likely something that has deeply affected you. As such, it is perfectly acceptable to write about them. If you overcame anorexia and started a peer outreach program at your high school for students with eating disorders, that would make a fine essay. If you were arrested for theft in ninth grade and then managed to turn your life around and ended up mentoring a younger friend, holding down a steady job, and raising your grades, that, too, makes compelling reading.

Tread carefully. In these cases an offhand remark about the difficulty you faced or superficial treatment of it can come off like a ploy for sympathy or whining. To avoid this, write unflinchingly about your problem, how it affected your life, how you managed to overcome it, and what you learned from it. "What does not kill us only makes us stronger," goes the old lie, but in this case, if you are going to include a difficulty, also include how fighting it has made you a better person.

Awful Essay Topic #524

"The day I realized I was smarter then everybody else."

The same thing goes for including anecdotes or topics that highlight your weaknesses. The essay (for the umpteenth time) is your chance to shine, not cast doubt over your ability and character. This said, including a section on a weakness or struggle can be a powerful weapon in your arsenal. That you are able to assess your own strengths and weaknesses indicates self-knowledge and intelligence; your willingness to write about them shows honesty, modesty, and more than a little bit of guts. All of these are traits that colleges love to see. Admissions officers are humans and are eager to see an applicant who is willing to admit he or she is an imperfect human who makes mistakes. Again, the trick is turning a weakness into a strength, without sounding whiny and without weakening the areas you have worked hard to build up in other parts of your application.

If this is the route you chose, beware of clichés. This type of essay can end up sounding corny in a hurry. Something like, "I really struggled in calculus. After getting a C first quarter, I studied every night, saw the teacher every night, and was tutored by my best friend, Bruce. Even though it would never be my best subject, I began to really like calculus and it taught me the value of hard work." This is superficial treatment of a topic that does not make the writer seem unique or memorable in any way.

More specific details, deeper analysis, and a more nuanced position are necessary. If there was a story about biting the erasers off pencils in frustration or about the textbook having a smiling clown on the cover who you could swear was mocking you—anything that distinguishes you from the multitudes of others who have struggled through the subject—then it might be interesting. Taking a view other than, "It was hard, but I learned a lot," would also be more compelling. Maybe as a French literature buff, you still don't see the point in integrals or as an aspiring engineer you realize that your potential career is going to be a lot harder than you thought it would be. In any event, this type of story works much better as a counterpoint to, or piece of, a bigger story. If you're writing about a stumbling block on the road to success, just make sure that you spend more time on the road than the stumble.

This is also a good time to lay out our philosophy on exaggerating or inventing difficulties in your life: don't do it—period. Not only is that unethical, it's probably not going to work. Admissions officers read essays for a living and like that high school English teacher everybody hated, they can detect bull at a range of fifteen miles and are authorized to shoot it down without warning. How interesting that your battle with polio goes unmentioned by any of your letters of recommendation and your interviewer. Don't screw around with that type of stuff. Enough said.

Back in the world of things you *should* be doing, there is the possibility that you've taken initiative and decided to create and answer your own question. Many colleges give this option and if you have a good idea, there's no reason you shouldn't write your own question.

Let's put emphasis on the word "question" because without a clear question, you're sunk and that's equally true if you're using a ready-made one. This is not to say that you can't simply sit

"Your English teacher may be helpful in editing your essay for grammar, but try to find someone who knows you better to help in developing a creative and personal topic."

—Sophomore, University of Minnesota

down and pound something out, then go back and see what you have—that might work fine in a first draft. But in a 500-word essay, you can't afford to waste any space, so at some point you need to focus your essay on a particular idea, theme, subject, object, or story. Physically writing out the question can be incredibly helpful—above all, it forces you to ask of each sentence and idea, "How does this answer the question? How is this relevant?" This ensures that you stay on topic and that those extraneous cute stories and pun-filled lines go where they really belong (painful as it is to admit) in the garbage.

If you chose your own question there are a few additional concerns. Of course you want passion for the topic and you want to make sure that it portrays you in a positive and unique way. You also have to make sure that your topic is about you and is of some significance. On the surface these don't seem like particularly weighty concerns, but they are things you need to be aware of in any admissions essay you write. Obviously the essay you're writing is about you and that's something to keep in mind if you're writing about someone else. If you've chosen to write about a personal hero or about a book that you love, that's terrific. Just don't make the mistake of giving them all the glory. Be sure to talk about why and how they inspire you, ways you disagree with them, anything that relates back to you. You're the one applying to college, not Uncle Fred, even if he's a war hero. Talk about your hero or movie or whatever, but be sure that it relates back to you in a coherent and carefully explained way.

In terms of weighty issues, you should also remember that while you don't have to solve world hunger in your essay, you also don't want to pick a frivolous topic. You need not pick *War and Peace* as your favorite book, but if you choose *Harold and the Purple Crayon*, an admissions officer may immediately question whether you take the application and the college you are applying to seriously. Again, if you have a fantastic and original idea, you might be able to get away with it, but odds are Harold is not connecting to a deeper issue, event, or philosophy that you want to discuss. You've spent most of your application building yourself up. Don't make yourself look like an intellectual lightweight with the essay.

The same thing goes for creative topics. If you want to write your essay as an ode in iambic pentameter or as stream of consciousness or as a short story, make sure you're good at it. While a safe, mediocre essay will not significantly advance your chances of admission, you may injure your chances with an entry that relies on a gimmick or is a sloppy excuse for a creative project. Admissions officers have seen whatever your brilliantly original idea is at least once before. You absolutely must be great if you attempt something outrageous. Then, you can gloat as you rack up points for guts and artistic talent. Sadly, most of us are not reliable judges of our own greatness. If you simply must do something in a non-essay format, run it past someone you trust— preferably several people, at least one of whom is a hopeless cynic (e.g. your freshman English teacher). If you get the seal of approval, go for it.

To write a great essay, you need a great topic. Any topic that excites you, paints you in a positive light, and has even a chance of making you stand out as a unique and fascinating individual is the right one.

General Essay Writing Advice

Your essay is evaluated on both content and presentation and for good reason. Effective writing skills are a key to success in college. If you can prove you are a clear and efficient communicator in your essay, that's one more reason for the admissions committee to like you. If, on the other hand, you can't produce a focused and comprehensible two-page essay, how can they realistically expect you to write a term paper ten times that size?

Although technically solid writing won't make up for an essay that dodges the question or chooses a lightweight topic or forgets that it's supposed to be about the applicant, it can make a good essay that much better.

The goal of this section is to help you present your ideas in a compelling way. Writing style should be the vehicle that carries forth your brilliant ideas, not the roadblock that holds them back.

Awful Essay Topic #367

"My Geometry teacher sucks because . . ."

A Picture Is Worth a Thousand Words

So that means you can only include half a picture in a 500-word essay, right? Not really. But while you're probably not going to include a photograph of Aunt Edna, you should strive to create pictures in the mind of your reader, at least in a verbal fashion. In order to do this, you will need concrete imagery.

Sound scary? It's not. All you need to do is be as specific as possible when you are describing something. Not only can you create a visual picture, but you invoke the other senses as well, making your essay that much more powerful. When you are attempting to describe something, try to think of interesting and specific details, even if at first they seem insignificant. These are the things that capture a reader's attention and make a situation seem real. Also ask yourself if there are any memorable sounds, tastes, or smells that you could throw in—the more senses you can engage, the more interesting your essay becomes.

Let's use the following sentence as an example:

> I read a really old copy of Robinson Crusoe for class. Some of the pages were missing and it was really dusty.

There is nothing wrong with these two sentences, and they are entirely correct grammatically. However, the very vague description does not conjure up any images in the reader's mind. Here is another version of the sentences:

> With a brown smudge on the title page and the cloth binding worn away along the spine, the copy of Robinson Crusoe I read for class was in terrible shape. Page 162 had been ripped out and when I slammed it shut, a cloud of dust tasting of salt coated my lips.

Because of the carefully chosen details sprinkled throughout the description, these sentences paint a more evocative picture than did the original. They grab the reader's attention with a variety of different images and sensations.

There can also be too much of a good thing of course. Take the following sentence:

> With a faded brown smudge on the title page the color of dried blood and the orange cloth binding worn away along the spine, the copy of Robinson Crusoe I read for junior English class was in terrible shape. Pages 162 through 180 had been ripped out and when I slammed it shut, a cloud of dust tasting of mildew and salt coated my lips.

In this example, the detail has been piled on too much, to the point where the reader has trouble focusing on a single image, sensation, or sentiment. It also doesn't ring true. If he was missing 19 pages, why didn't he spring for a complete copy from a used bookstore for 99 cents? Did the writer actually sit and savor the taste of the floating dust so much so that he could distinguish between its different ingredients? Be sensitive to detail but do not go overboard to the point of exaggeration.

Danger!

Yes, it's time again for a rant, this time aimed at a few stylistic no-nos.

There is an initial propensity to employ Gordian conglomerates of laughably loquacious language and asinine alliteration. In other words, if you use ridiculous vocabulary, you will end up with gobbledy-gook. Just write simply. This is not an excuse to write crudely or vaguely, but all those big words you found reading the dictionary to prepare for the SAT have no place in your essay. Your ability to use your computer's thesaurus impresses no one, and even worse, you can end up saying something other than what you mean. Do not talk about the entomology of a word, when you obviously mean *etymology*. One is the study of insects, the other the history of words. There's nothing worse than a word that's supposed to make you look smart making you look dumb.

Another danger to be avoided is over self-promotion. This is another one of those situations in which you need to strike a balance between making the strongest case possible and coming across as a shrill narcissist unable to see your own faults. In general, it's best to let other people—your letter-writers and interviewer—brag for you. It's crucial that you present all the facts, and that's why there's a place for awards and activities on the application. But, it's generally best to let the facts speak for themselves. If your essay involves an honor or activity, that's great, but don't use it as an excuse to gloat or insert a list of your leadership positions. Avoid an inferiority complex but be humble. Think of Michael Jordan—there's no need to go around screaming you're the best when you already know it. You *are* Michael Jordan after all.

Remember also to avoid clichés. The life lessons that you learned from early childhood fables were also part of everyone else's formative years, and they don't show deep insight or profound understanding of anything except common knowledge. Some common clichés to avoid:

Winning isn't everything.

Don't judge a book by its cover.

It's important to be yourself.

There are hundreds of others, but these are just a few to get you thinking. Read your essay and ask yourself what your main point is. If it's something that easily lends itself to a common adage, time to think harder, dig deeper, and revise!

Words, Words, Words: On Diction and Syntax

Eeew, gross, right? Thought you had managed to escape that? Never. While this section isn't meant to make up for sleeping through three years of English class, it does hit on a few of the high points from the beloved land of word choice and sentence construction.

Be concise. That's a big deal, especially in an essay this short. Your goal is to deliver your full meaning in as few words as possible. You are defeated when you start cutting words you need, but if you can trim away the fat, the essay will be clearer and more forceful.

One of the most effective ways of shortening sentences is by using the active voice. The active voice (we're sure you already know this, but just in case) is where the subject of the sentence is doing the action, rather than having it done to it, which is the passive voice. Compare, "The dog was given to me by my Uncle," to

Awful Essay Topic #83

"And another thing, I don't need your freaking school!"

"My Uncle gave me the dog." The second sentence is shorter and avoids using the verb in the passive tense. Writing with vivid, active verbs is one of the most important things you can do. (Or instead, "Vivid, active verbs lend zest to your prose." See the difference?) Be wary of verbs like "ate" when you could use "devoured," "put" when you could use "threw," or "said," when you could use "screamed." Just look (scan) through your verbs and see (discern) if there are ways you could make the action more definite or forceful in the reader's mind.

Look to combine sentences wherever possible. There is always the dangerous tendency for writers to produce sentences that all sound the same, which is boring to read and de-emphasizes your important points. If the writing takes on a repetitive sounding cadence, the reader

will be lulled into not caring by the time you get to the important parts. And how would the reader know which ideas are
more important if they all sound the same? If every sentence
seems to begin with "I," rework or combine a few to offer your
reader some variety. Example: "I really loved my uncle. I used
to visit him every day. I was shocked and confused when he
moved." By the time we read the third sentence, the repetition
of "I," coupled with the consistent sentence length has left the
idea of the uncle moving with little to no power. Try: "I used to
love visiting my uncle at his old house any day I could make it up
there. At four years old, it was impossible to comprehend what
had happened when he left. Why did he move away?" This construction uses sentence and subject variety in a more effective
way—and even uses short sentence length in the last question to
evoke the voice of the confused four-year-old. Not too shabby.
You, too, should think about the sentences that contain the
most important or moving ideas of your essay. You may want to
think about specially crafting these sentences outside of the
body of the text, and then working them in. One particularly
effective strategy is creating what's known as a periodic sentence; one in which the main thought comes last. Example:
"After returning home from an hour in the snow, covered in
white and chilled to the bone, I realized I had forgotten my little
brother." See how the periodic sentence is building toward the
most important part, and because of that, it gets a little bit extra
emphasis. We don't really talk or write like that all the time, so
this is another special technique to be used sparingly. But if

used effectively, it's a good way to create varied sentence structure and highlight certain ideas.

Furthermore, look to cut pathetic excuses for transitions. "Furthermore," for instance. Sometimes these transitions do the trick, but not if they are tacked on in an illogical fashion. If you read down your essay and see each new paragraph beginning with "Moreover," or "Meanwhile," or "In conclusion" (that last one is especially trite sounding), ask yourself if there isn't a better way to introduce those ideas without sounding like a third-grade book report.

If you use these sort of basic or modular transitions, you show an unwillingness to creatively segue. (Silly rabbit, modular segues are for kids!) Make up a real transition or do without the transition entirely. "Look to cut pathetic excuses for transitions," is blunt, but it is a perfectly clear topic sentence. You could also try opening a new idea with a word that will help either grab the reader's attention, or encapsulate the idea that's coming. "Bravery is going into the fray without armor." The author is about to talk about bravery. "Obsession and love are very different things." The author will, hopefully without frightening the reader, explain such a sentiment. These types of transitions give the essay more pizzazz, as well as elevate it to a higher caliber of writing. The admissions people will appreciate the added sparkle these can give your writing.

This is a lot to remember. The good news is you can go back and fix what doesn't work when you revise, but the more you take care of now, the better. So get to it! Be original, be concise, and be confident. Manage to do that, and you're well on your way to writing an excellent essay.

Still need some guidance? We've selected some essays for you to peruse, and we've included some criticisms to help you see some basic errors and some shining examples that are out there in the college essay world.

Sample Essay #1: My Future

Shoes that squeak. The roar of the crowd. The bounce of the ball. These are just some of the things you will here at a women's tennis game. I have played varsity tennis for two years at Jefferson High School and before that I was on JV, too. I think tennis was one of the best things I did in high school because it taught me the value of working hard and that teamwork is of importance.

It wasn't always easy though. My junior year I sprained my knee and had to have physical therapy. The doctors and nurses helped me a lot and were very nice. They inspired me, because now I want to be a physical therapist too. I think that they have one of the most important jobs because they are able to help people. I always try to help my family and friends whenever I can, so I think I would be really good at it. For example, I helped my boyfriend find a job, and now we're so much in love that he wants to go to college, too. Also I have been hurt, so I would know how it feels.

I have also done many other things in high school, like art club, singing in the choir and "The Write Stuff," our school newspaper. Even though it was not always easy to do all of this and still get my homework done, I learned a lot and had fun. We were also pretty successful because the choir went to state two years in a row and won the spirit award.

I was not always a great student, but that changed near the end of my junior year. After one really bad math test, my math teacher, Mr. Murphy, took me aside and told me that I could be doing a lot better if I would spend more time working on it. He really inspired me and was very patient. Each day after school he would spend time with me helping me with trigonometry. Thanks to him, I learned that learning is not only important to my future but can also be fun and exciting. This is something I will always remember that will inspire me in college if I ever have a hard time.

I am more than just an innumerable list of activities. I am a person worried about my friends and the people around me. Just like Mr. Murphy, I now help some of my friends with math homework after school. I tutor my boyfriend in Algebra everyday. We don't always get the right answers, but we make learning fun and exciting, like he does. I am taking this new attitude into all my classes this year and getting good grades.

I am also a person who can be a leader. In the summer I taught tennis lessons to seven-year olds as a part of the City Recreation Department. They came in not knowing anything about tennis and left understanding the basics and having a lot of fun. I also volunteer at the County Homeless Shelter every week and became the Youth District Assistant Coordinator. This has been a rewarding way of improving my community while meeting many wonderful people and breaking down stereotypes.

In conclusion, I hope that you feel that you have a better knowledge of me. A definition of my life would be that to be diligent, ebullient, and scrupulous is a cause of success and enjoyment of life. I hope that I can persist in having this attitude in college and that it will assist in the career I aspire to.

Critique of Essay #1

A wise man once said, "Learn from other people's mistakes. You'll never have time to make them all yourself."

The biggest problem with this essay is the lack of focus. After reading it, we have no definitive idea of what question it is answering. "Please talk at random about yourself" is a good guess. There is no central theme or thought or topic, no one thing that all the anecdotes and information build up to. This is a fatal mistake. What is this essay really about? The author's plans for her future, her favorite high school activities, an inspirational teacher, and community service all parade on through, but has she illustrated who she really is? If you were an admissions officer, would it strike you as memorable in any way? When the time comes for the committee to accept or reject, would you say, "This student really made an impression on me with that essay she wrote on, umm, what was it again?"

Paragraph 1

HOOK 'EM. You want an attention-grabber at the beginning of your essay, but a couple of sound effects like this are more at home in a junior high school newspaper. Even a corny hook, like real sound effects ("Bang! Thwock! Roar!" Sounds like an episode of Batman, but it's an improvement) or even something fairly conventional and straightforward ("Spraining my knee was one of the best things that ever happened to me") would work. Anything that captures readers' attention, draws them in, and makes them want to read more is great.

PARALLEL POWER. Though the writer's biggest problem is content, there are some technical problems that should be addressed. One repeated problem deals with parallel structure. A sentence with parallel structure would read, "My bird is blue, fat, and noisy." One without it might be, "My bird is blue, he appears to be overweight, and he is noisy to listen to." The first sentence is a more efficient and striking way of delivering information. The final sentence (try "the value of hard work and the importance of teamwork" rather than "the value of working hard and that teamwork is of importance") lacks parallel structure and is weaker for it.

TRY NOT TO USE "I THINK." Of course you think it, you're writing it for crying out loud! The same goes for "In my opinion." Of course it's your opinion. Whom else's opinion would you be expressing? Extra words make your style slushy instead of crisp.

SPELL CHECK WILL NOT CATCH ALL YOUR MISTAKES!
In line 2, "here" is used in place of "hear." Not a big mistake, but one that makes ewe look foolish nevertheless.

UNSUPPORTED AND GENERIC SENTENCES ARE BORING. Take the one about tennis teaching the author about hard work and teamwork. Gosh, it's just what we were expecting to hear—what makes it interesting? Is there some supporting evidence or a neat story that will make this anything but an empty platitude?

Paragraph 2

DON'T USE VERY. DON'T USE NICE. DON'T USE FUN. Say what you mean! Better yet, find a noun or verb that means precisely what you want it to. Instead of "very nice" or even "extremely nice," the author should explain that the nurses were willing to answer questions about her operation, or that the doctor hummed the 1812 Overture to take her mind off the pain. "Nice" and "fun," as well as the author's other favorite, "inspiring," are unspecific words that are stripped of any precise or interesting meaning.

DON'T MAKE YOUR READER SAY, "WELL, DUH!" Doctors are important because they help people? How fascinating. So do the guys cooking burgers at Wendy's. You know what it feels like to be hurt? So does everybody else. Overstating the obvious does not make you look smart. The writer is explaining why she wants to become a physical therapist, a profession that requires years of difficult and expensive education, but gives us no deeper reason than that she wants to help people and no evidence that she could be successful, unless you count her own injury. If the author were to focus on this, she would want to elaborate more on why she is interested in this profession and what skills and experience she possesses that have prepared her for it.

Paragraph 3

WHERE HAVE I SEEN THIS BEFORE? Great, a list of high school activities. Odds are there's one somewhere else in the application. Since the author gives no details on any of the activities in the essay, they serve no purpose there. If you want to wax poetic on the art club, that's a fine subject for an essay. A series of lists is not. This paragraph could be deleted and the essay loses nothing.

Paragraph 4

HONESTY IS NICE . . . The anecdote with the teacher is about as close as this essay gets to a nice, specific, memorable incident. It's also gutsy in that the author admits to weakness—she needed extra help in math. Everyone has struggled with some course before, so we all understand and empathize with the author. We bond. We feel as though we might be able to understand the writer a little better.

. . . SHOOTING YOURSELF IN THE FOOT IS NOT. The teacher suggests the author is failing because she is lazy. This is something you want to put delicately, even if your teacher didn't. At the very least you'd want to include a rebuttal in the essay. The whole point of the essay is to paint yourself in the best light. Putting your work ethic in question fails to do this.

Paragraph 5

PET PEEVE. Innumerable activities? There were three or four the last time I checked. Innumerable suggests something you *can't* put a number on. The author could get away with *numerous*, but her attempt to use a word she didn't fully understand looks foolish. A few other common screwed-up words: loose (not tight) versus lose (not winning). Affect versus effect. If you *affect* something, you exert a force on it, you change it in some way. An effect is a result of that change. The earth is *affected* by increased levels of carbon dioxide. An *effect* of this is global warming. Imply (to suggest) versus infer (to look at evidence and draw a conclusion.) My math teacher *implies* that I am

"My first college essay was incredibly boring because I tried to write what I thought admissions officers would want to hear. When I asked my friends and family what really stood out about me, I came up with a great topic and a much improved essay."

—Junior, University of Wisconsin

stupid by saying I can't even add. I *infer* that he has self-esteem problems because he insults his students.

MORE FOOT SHOOTING. OK, so the author's study group and boyfriend don't always get the right answer—does she need to advertise it? If so, rather than saying, "We do not always get the right answers," she might try something like, "Though we're sometimes frustrated," or "We spend hours scratching our heads over more difficult problems." Oh yeah, and it's often a bad idea to mention your significant other in your college essay. No matter how much you say you're in love, admissions officers don't want to hear about it. It comes off sounding like something you want to brag about or just can't shut up about. Either way, it's bad form. Leave them out of these 500 words. You'll thank us in a year.

Paragraph 6

BE CONCISE. This essay is about 580 words long. Revising individual sentences might shave off 200 words. Case in point: "I am a person who can be a leader." Hmm, were we thinking the author wasn't a person? This reduces the sentence to "I also can be a leader." Why use the weak "can be" formation? "I am a leader." This is a more forceful configuration of the same sentence and takes up half the space. There are dozens of places where similar revisions should be made. Sticking to the 500-word limit isn't vital, but around there is about right. Admissions officers will hate you right away if your essay takes too long to even finish, but they don't count words, so that 501st word can stay put without worry.

PLEASE: ANECDOTES AND EXAMPLES. Are there no poignant or cute or funny stories about teaching seven-year-olds tennis? Are those "rewarding" days that are filled with "interesting people" really so boring that the author can't share any of it with us? This is the stuff a glorious essay is made of—specific, original stories—and it's left out. What does a Youth District Assistant Coordinator do? Which stereotypes were broken down? Any of that could make for fascinating reading.

Paragraph 7

DO NOT USE "IN CONCLUSION." Or "Finally." These generic transitions have all the appeal of a Velcro hood ornament. We can see the end of the essay, don't waste space by telling us it's coming.

USE THE ACTIVE VOICE. Occupying the place where we would normally find the best written sentence of the entire essay, the one that clinches the essay right at the end, we find this: "A definition of my life would be that to be diligent, ebullient, and scrupulous is a cause of success and enjoyment of life." Setting aside the fact that this statement is virtually meaningless or depressingly unoriginal ("Hard work makes me happy and successful!"), it is poorly written. There are three forms of "is" in there, the harbinger of the passive voice. Try rewriting the sentence like this: "Diligence, ebullience, and persistence define my life and give me joy and success." Not great, but better. It's also hard to hide BS in the active voice, so converting your passive to active can help you spot pieces of your essay that need to be improved or reworked.

Awful Essay Topic #498

"Your school is *totally* not my last choice."

IF YOU'RE GONNA USE A BIG WORD, KNOW WHAT IT MEANS.

Do all those hundred-dollar words in the last paragraph look out of place in a two-bit essay? Was someone hitting the old "thesaurus" menu option in an attempt to look smarter? George Orwell once wrote: "Never use a long word when a shorter one will convey the same meaning." If there's a long word, like diligence, which has a nuanced meaning that you really want, go for it. (Diligent and hard working are as different as fudge and chocolate.) Don't screw up. Look at the last sentence. Two mistakes in the last two words. One, a sentence ends in a preposition—not as heinous a crime as it used to be, but still a no-no if it can be avoided. Second, the writer is aspirating a career. If you aspirate something you inhale it into your lungs. One aspires to a career, but does not aspirate it.

Given that the author is interested in a medical career, this type of error, especially in the last two words, suggests that she is an intellectual lightweight.

Final Diagnosis

Not much here. In an attempt to talk about a lot of things vaguely, the author covers none of it well. If she had focused and included specific, unique information on any one of the many topics she covers, the essay would be much stronger.

Sample Essay #2

(This One's Real, Folks, So Pay Attention!)

A Corner of One's Own

When I draw, paint, or sculpt, I like to think that my brain metamorphoses from a pile of gelatinous gray goo into a dome of richly stained glass where light bounces and reflects. The urgency of capturing and subduing each shaft of color intensifies the sensation of my nerves, making them distinct workers that speed power along a circuit of energy condensing at my lower back (that funny place that aches if you sit too long) and pouring out my fingertips. My face expresses this experience. With the weight of a paintbrush or pastel in my hand, my lips purse, my eyes squint, my nose scrunches, and my arms wave as though conducting a manic symphony. Just the pungent smell of charcoal or mellow scent of oil paint lifts the weight of reality into a world of color, light, and form.

To make settling my artistic cravings more convenient, I petitioned for an easel as my Christmas gift two years ago. On a little patch of gray cement I cleared out in the corner of the garage, I would squint through the flickering florescent light to transform lumps of pigment into image and texture. Even when the chill of El Nino made the garage more suitable for storing meat than for storing me, I would still troop out, armed with my "uniform"—two pairs of socks, slippers, a couple of shirts, a sweater, long johns, sweats, and my dad's old jeans. While the outfit did bulletproof me in case of siege, I had the range of motion of a swaddled baby and only narrowly averted tragedy on several emergency bathroom breaks.

The addition of a heat dish made my corner inhabitable for human life forms and awakened some odd combination of female nesting instinct and artistic passion; in other words, I felt the need to accessorize. Digging around in the garage, I discovered a worn rug that time and better decorating sense had buried under a pile of battered suitcases. Softer and warmer than the cement floor, it cushions my feet, grounds my artistic frenzy, and pays homage to the last days of disco. Tired of stooping to the ground to grab my supplies, I foraged some more and discovered the white desk that my legs stopped fitting under years ago. My tools at my fingertips, I can attack my canvases with uninterrupted focus. If my energy flags, I pump up the volume of the tired-looking radio that I rescued from eternal garage exile. Listening to the buzz of music, by the light of the tubby lamp with the cracked shade, I find inspiration.

Sometimes, when an idea presses at my fingertips, frustrated by the monotony of brush cleaning, I scoop up paint with my hands and smear it onto the canvas like a crazed lunch lady pressing the slop into Sloppy Joes. Emboldened by an excellent dental plan, I bite off the stubborn tops to tubes of paint and squirt color directly onto canvas. Only in the security of my corner can I splatter, sing, flail, and make as many goofy faces as I like. Amongst the boxes, old Halloween costumes, lawnmower, trashcans, and general clutter of our house, I have established a clearing of about 3 feet by 4 feet that belongs to me.

Critique of Essay #2

This is a well done essay about a relatively standard topic. At times it takes itself too seriously, using long words and phrases when shorter ones would clearly get the message across, and a number of passages get bogged down with extra words. But the overall effect of this essay is still very good. It certainly worked for the person who wrote it, and here's why:

CONCRETE SENSORY IMAGERY. How many college essays contain smells or tactile images? Here we have charcoal and oil paints, we get a wonderfully squishy feeling in our fingertips at the suggestion of "a pile of gelatinous gray goo" and in the description of squashing paint into the canvas the way we might Sloppy Joes. Departing from this, the author evokes nicely the chill of the garage with a list that piles on words the same way the author has piled on clothes. These pieces are fun to read and evocative. We are far more likely to remember something if we have a sensory experience to add to it rather than trying to remember an abstraction alone.

SPECIFIC DETAILS. What if the author had described the garage as cluttered or herself as wearing a lot of clothes? Are either of these nearly as interesting as the long lists of stuff (socks, slippers, and long johns; Halloween costumes, lawnmowers, and trashcans)? Specific details bring a story to life, they focus our attention on a specific object and allow us to imagine it. This is good stuff.

ACTION VERBS ARE WELL USED. Look at the sentence in which the author begins to paint in earnest. She does not sit passively, but "splatters," "sings," and "flails." She does not merely look or get or find, she "digs," "stoops," "grabs," or "forages." Action verbs draw in a reader. After reading essays all day long comprised mostly of "am," "is," and "are," you'd want to fling something, too.

As always, there are a few things that might have been handled differently:

A BIT OVER THE TOP? Even the attempts at humor are written in the high-flown style that permeates this piece, leaving some readers saying, "Hey, lighten up." Painting is probably not a transcendental experience all the time. Even the title, adapted from a Virginia Woolf essay, contributes to the overall tone of seriousness and academic snobbery.

A LOVE AFFAIR WITH LANGUAGE. OK already, we get the point: the writer either has a huge vocabulary or has taken an extraordinary amount of time writing this essay. Not that either one is a bad thing—the admissions essay is a chance to show off— but at times there is simply too much. Write simply, write beautifully, and write briefly. It is possible that you, like this author, will use all your big words correctly, but it's an unnecessary risk and makes what in places could be a profoundly simple and easy-to-read essay overblown.

Despite these criticisms, it's still a solid essay. If the author were borderline it might not be enough to push her over the line, but it would certainly complement a strong and well-rounded application.

Sample Essay #3

(Another Real One That Worked)

On the Lighter Side

Spring is a happy season. It is the time when flowers bloom, couples wed, children smile, and the world collectively sneezes, sending the waste of winter scattering. These rejected particles of wintry melancholy, not content to spend three seasons bandying about the Jet Stream, gently waft toward the surface of the earth, and settle on the walls of American high schools—as Student Government campaign posters. School elections are traditionally dominated by those who began their careers handing out

Cheerios in the sandbox, aspiring to establish themselves as those who would be responsible for their school's annual predetermined activities. While most students, come springtime, would be hard pressed to identify any accomplishment of the incumbent Student Government, the electorate as a whole does not hesitate to reelect overwhelmingly the same officers year after year. Those who boycott the vote, disillusioned altogether with the process and its überclass, view the proceedings with much the same attitude granted toward Microsoft and the income tax; they revile the institution's ills, and yet realize their perspective might be different had they gotten on the bandwagon earlier. It is a pattern so ingrained as to inspire the most widely accepted recognition of American stereotype, a Hollywood movie. Under the surface, however, it begs to be challenged, and it was this challenge that I, who had never before run for a school-wide office, accepted when I declared my candidacy for Student Government President.

Whether I was truly motivated by a subconscious desire to prove the system wrong or a genuine urge to make a difference in my school remains in question. To me, the challenge of uniting a diverse student body through seriousness and humor seemed both daunting and appealing. Initially inhibited by a school rule that prohibited speech-making, I turned to the printed word. I first sought to highlight my public school's ethnic diversity by reaching out to the approximate third of my school of Latino descent, who, if the attitude evident in my AP Spanish class was any indication, traditionally had shown their appreci-

ation for the week-long campaign by forgetting to vote. My largest poster proclaimed that "The best candidate for Student
Government President *se llama Roberto,*" and featured the
grinning visage of the South American pack animal. Without
leaving the animal kingdom, I also tried to shake English-
speakers from their springtime apathy with a placard that read
"Vote for Robert Dubbin—He won't take no carp from nobody"
and featured a colorful picture of a fish. It was when I was
approached by a complete stranger, who first asked whether I
was "Se Llama," and then asked for a "carp" sign, that I realized my strategy had struck a responsive chord in a student
body jaded by years of generic advertising.

My competitors for the presidency, as fate (and Hollywood)
would have it, consisted of two archetypal individuals—a cheerleader and a football player. The preliminary elections resulted in
a runoff election between the cheerleader and me, and I
received many subsequent congratulations and pats on the back
from my loyal supporters. By my assessment, if my dedicated
throng of supporters were to turn out for the runoff in the same
numbers as the preliminary, and I inherited the football player's
votes with the help of my track teammates, victory would be
assured! This flight of fancy might have been realized, had there
not been one tiny snag: it is an unwritten rule, or tradition if you
will, that nobody votes in runoff elections. While my friends and
those who had supported me from the beginning turned out to
vote, it seemed those who I had recruited through advertisement
simply sat glued to their lunch tables. That afternoon, an imper-

sonal recorded message informed me that my campaign for Student Government President had ended in defeat.

The proverbial agony of defeat soon subsided in favor of a more optimistic outlook. My modest effort to overcome the ills of the Student Government had shaken, however slightly, the stronghold occupied by the forces of apathy. The election made me realize that the Student Government seemed inaccessible only because no one had dared to challenge it; it took only small doses of resolve and humor to break the misconception. Unfortunately, as I discovered, humor and resolve will only take you so far in overcoming convention. The experience of my high school campaign has taught me the invaluable life lesson that cleverness alone is not a substitute for getting your foot in the right doors at the right times. That's why, when it comes to extracurricular possibilities in college, I'll be sure to plan ahead and line up the necessary support before I grab a handful of Cheerios, toss them up into the Jet Stream—and start a software company.

Critique of Essay #3

On the whole, this is a well-written essay. The laid-back, slightly playful tone is engaging. If you put yourself in the position of the admissions officer, who has to read a couple dozen essays a day, a funny and unusual essay would have its appeal. This is more wry than it is laugh-out-loud funny, but it's different enough from most other essays that it stands out.

Initially, this essay doesn't appear to be packed with information. Look for facts here and you'll find only that the author launched an unsuccessful student council campaign and that he speaks some Spanish. That's fine. An essay shouldn't be one more chance for you to make a laundry list of activities or skills. What this essay does do well is tell a complete and interesting story. It is in the way the story is told that we learn the most about the author. He is witty, willing to question convention and his own motivations, able to admit to weakness, and wields the English language with confidence.

Still, this is just one piece of an application. If there were multiple essays, the author might have tried a more serious tack in the other ones, or perhaps in any short-answer questions, to balance out the unusual tone of this piece. Here are a few other comments on this essay.

The author gets away with his elaborate sentences because he doesn't take them too seriously. Normally if someone were to write, "the electorate as a whole does not hesitate to reelect overwhelmingly the same officers," or "Those who boycott the vote, disillusioned with the process and its überclass . . ." it would come across as incredibly pompous. This author manages to get away with it because (1) he uses all his words correctly (2) the tone of this essay is mocking rather than deadly serious. We can easily imagine what the author would like to say: "Those idiot kids keep voting for the same do-nothing candidates every year" and the length to which he goes to avoid saying this is amusing.

Awful Essay Topic #112

"My last name is on your new gymnasium."

THE PROBLEM WITH HUMOR . . .

is that not everyone gets it. It's gutsy to even try it, so if you didn't think it was funny, you've gotta give this guy mad props for trying, right?

THERE'S HONESTY HERE. The first sentence of the second paragraph is particularly intriguing ("Whether I was truly motivated by a subconscious desire to prove the system wrong or a genuine urge to make a difference in my school remains in question"). It would be far easier for the writer to pat himself on the back and pass off his motives as purely high-minded. The author falls into this more comfortable position in the next sentence (although, do we honestly believe anyone who says he's running for "the challenge of uniting a diverse student body?"). It would have been intriguing had he stayed on the guiltier strand for a while, talking about running for the wrong reasons, but getting us to sympathize with him anyway.

THE FUN IS IN THE DETAILS. Notice that the author does not say, "I campaigned with various humorous posters." He's up front with providing specific details. These are fun to read and the llama thing is far more memorable than telling us that you're funny in the abstract.

THE LENGTH IS GOOD. Did you notice or did it bother you that this essay is nearly 800 words long? The beginning and end could be more efficiently worded, but the author does a nice job of taking his time developing the story. Putting a lot of pressure on yourself to finish in exactly 500 words is destructive. As we've said, admissions officers won't care if you go a bit over, though an extra 300 words is beginning to push the boundaries of good taste.

OUR LAST WORDS ON THIS ESSAY: Leave out the universals. The reflections on springtime and the political process in general at the beginning and end of this essay seem out of place, especially considering the more lighthearted tone of the rest of the essay. There's a real temptation to try to make yourself sound deep by including seemingly stunning observations about the big lesson that this incident taught you, or about how it proved a universal truth. Hopefully your essay is good enough that the reader can draw his or her own conclusions about these things. Had this essay had a tighter focus on the incident it discusses, it would have been stronger. But we liked it—that's why it's here . . . and the people in admissions liked it, too. Good job.

Reviseing and Pruefreeding You're Essay

It is now time for the single most important piece of essay writing advice you'll ever receive: start early. Kinda ironic we waited until now to tell you, isn't it? What's that? It's due tomorrow? Join the club.

To be perfectly honest you'll want to write your essay *at minimum* a couple of weeks before it's due and you should probably mull over potential topics for a long time before that. The added time gives you a chance to set your essay aside for a while and come back to it. If, after a couple of days, you take another look at the essay and wonder what you were on when you wrote it, good thing you double-checked. On the other hand, if it's not nearly as bad as you feared, you can breathe a sigh of relief and work on making it sparkle.

Your first priority is revising for content. Start by rereading the question. If, while trying to answer it, you've wandered and digressed, then thinking about the question is where you'll need to start. Ask yourself how each sentence advances your essay, how it is related to the topic. When there is no immediate answer or the answer involves a particularly circuitous path of logic ("I was treasurer of Spanish club, which shows I know a lot about money, and I'll have money if I'm a doctor, and I want to be a doctor because I like chemistry..."), cut it.

Your two best friends in the revisions are DELETE and BACK-SPACE. Be ruthless with your cutting. This will free up space if you are running long, which you can use to expand on strong sections or pump up anemic ones. Even if you're stumped and it's due tomorrow, far better to turn in a tightly written, coherent 300-word essay than one bloated with irrelevant prattle.

One method of cutting involves hitting adverbs particularly hard. If you're attempting to describe something and those descriptors give you good mileage, then keep them. But be especially aware of waffling with extra ones, for example, "Perhaps the most important experience of my life was not unlike the nearly overwhelming, awelike experience of attending my first opera." There are (at least) two things wrong with this sentence. First, the author likes opera, though it might be difficult to tell. Second, like most politicians, it wants everything both ways. Was it the most important experience of

"My college essay ran so long that the first draft was in eight point font with quarter inch margins. Thank God my printer ran out of ink or I wouldn't have even thought of revising. I might have had to send a reading glass with the application!

—Sophomore, Rutgers University

your life or not? "Perhaps," "maybe," and "somewhat" do nothing for your writing and should be cut out. Doing so will make your writing clearer, more efficient and, darn it, it will sound as if you actually have an opinion on something. If the experience was not unlike something, then what *was* it like? Is a not unfun movie fun, or is it something else? Is a not unbrown dog brown? Be specific— explain exactly what something is or is not like, and don't cop out. If something is almost awe-inspiring, then what is it? Is it merely inspirational, downright disappointing, or is it, after all, awe- inspiring? Any one of these would be a better choice than the wimpy "not un-" formation.

Once you're satisfied with the content of your essay, begin to revise individual sentences with regard to the stylistic sugges- tions we offered earlier. Look to be as concise as possible, vary your sentence structure to enhance interest, and avoid the icky pitfalls mentioned above. If your computer has a spell and grammar checker, by all means run them more than once. Try reading your essay aloud. By actually forcing yourself to read closely what you've written, awkward phrasings, missing words, and repeated fragments and repeated fragments jump off the page at you.

Only after doing all of this, take your essay to an esteemed col- league for help. A lot of people could play this part—a friend who is an excellent writer, a parent, or a guidance counselor familiar with college essays. And there is, of course, the most hallowed resource of all: the English teacher. I mean, let's face it, these guys read and correct essays for a living and can help you out big time with creating a consistent tone and style, keeping you on topic and telling you what does and doesn't work. If you have an English teacher, or any teacher at all, you feel comfortable with and who knows you well, he or she would be an excellent person to talk to. By doing as much as you are able on your own, you show respect for the poor sap who's about to take a couple hours out of his or her life to help you out. There's nothing worse than sitting down with someone you respect only to notice that you've made four mistakes in the first sentence, except for never catching them at all.

An outside perspective is useful for more than just grammar and style. Sometimes that line you thought was hysterical flops in front of a live audience. Real conversation:

Teacher: What is this pun doing here?

Applicant: It makes me sound witty and smart.

Teacher: That's why it will be so hard to cut from the final draft.

This is a polite way of saying, "Not by a long shot, bucko." We all need someone to tell us that sometimes. The most ornate lines are often so complicated because there's nothing underneath them, or because you're blathering on about nothing. Come down hardest on your favorite sentences.

Your marvelous assistant, if he or she knows you well, can also tell you if the essay does you justice. Maybe you've left out your sense of humor or compassion or love of life. Maybe you've done so on purpose, but give their suggestions some serious thought.

Don't hesitate to get help at multiple points during the essay writing process from multiple people. If you're stumped a half-

The book *The Education of Robert Nifkin* by Daniel Pinkwater, which tells the story of a high school senior and his interactions with the crazy people in his school, is written in the form of a college application essay.

page into it, do all you can and talk it over with someone. A brainstorming session with a friend or teacher can make all the difference early on. Don't be shy about going back for a second round of revisions either. If you're writing quality stuff, a teacher should be glad to read it. Your friends will tolerate it because they like you.

A Word of Caution

There is such a thing as too much help. One of the most common and vehement complaints of admissions officers is that essays have the life sucked out of them by too many rounds of polishing. Your parents—bless their souls, they're just trying to help—have a tendency to be the worst offenders. You may have heard the story of the girl who thought she was dictating her essay to her mother, when good old Mom was actually writing something completely different. This is an obvious and extreme case, but there tend to be subtle pressures from your helpers—certainly this is not limited to parents—to move away from crisp, clear prose. Use a longer word here, rephrase this, for gosh sakes, don't talk about *that*, and all of a sudden, the energetic and unique essay that you had has been reduced to something that someone else thinks someone in the admissions office wants to see. Since admissions officers like a different, honest, even slightly rough-edged essay, polishing one to a blindingly conventional sheen is counter-productive.

Use your helpers for brainstorming, advice, and editing help, but at all costs retain creative control over the essay. You should be showing off a work in progress, maybe even asking them some specific questions, *not* writing with someone looking over your shoulder.

When you've got what you think is a finished product, spend a little more time reading it very slowly. Double-check names of people or places, which you may have skipped with the spell-checker. Print out a copy and read that. For whatever reason, the human brain is more adept at picking out mistakes on a sheet of paper than on a screen. This is also a great chance to have Mom read through one last time, if nothing else to make sure you've spelled your name correctly and to make sure you haven't done anything really stupid like saying you think Yale will be the perfect school for you in your application to Harvard.

An urban legend? It really does happen, and while some admissions officers are willing to laugh it off, others take it as an insult or at least an indicator that they are not your top choice and will treat your application accordingly. Don't be the one they remember this year.

Print out your final copy. Make sure it's legible and that the ink hasn't smeared all over the place. There's no need to use expensive paper, but unlike the guy who decided to stand out by using fluorescent yellow, do use white. Stack it neatly with your application and breathe a satisfied sigh of relief.

CHAPTER SEVEN

Face-off

The Interview

We told you that the college essay was your big chance to demonstrate your personality to the admissions committee—to demonstrate in elegant prose the funky and fabulous youness of you. Well, the personal interview is your second shot at showcasing, now in living color, just how wonderful you really are.

The problems associated with using interviews as a fair way to evaluate candidates has caused a lot of schools to downplay their importance. Over the years most colleges have phased out the interview as a required piece of the application package. Stanford and the University of New Hampshire have never interviewed, and Providence College and Stonehill College nixed them from the application process years ago. Colleges like Princeton and Northwestern only recommend interviews, but most students opt to talk—70 percent of Princeton applicants sign up. Don't take this as an invitation to ignore the interview as unimportant. Not only do some schools, like Harvard, Yale, and MIT, still try their darnedest to interview every applicant, going to that "optional" interview shows a commitment to the application process of the school that can only help you in the admissions game.

The interview is an entirely different species of expression in the wild jungle of college admissions. It demands the same qualities that the college essay does, seeking out the unique, articulate, enthusiastic, focused, and otherwise brilliant from the applicant pack, but in a much more intimate (and often more intimidating) environment of spontaneity. In other words, you've got the chance to strut your stuff more effectively but with a greater risk of goofing up. While in the interview, you don't have to agonize over every semicolon and metaphor as you do in your writing, you also lose the power to carefully craft (and revise) the impression that you give the interviewer.

What's more, tons of other things influence an interview that would never come into play with an essay. Bad breath will only hurt you in your writing if you lick the paper. The people who read your essays will never know if you have sweaty palms or a lisp. So much immediate pressure to make a good impression can tear at your nerves, but if you use the unique nature of the interview to your advantage, you can score serious points.

So don't freak out when you interview. Not only is "psycho" generally not one of the qualities that colleges look for, but out of all the pieces of the application puzzle, the interview has the highest potential for actually being enjoyable. Unless standardized testing puts the feather in your cap, interacting with a (usually) friendly person who knows and loves the school you're considering can focus your decision and serve as a great pump for the college experience. As your only shot at an on-the-record dialogue with the admissions crew, the interview allows you, for better or for worse, to clarify their impression of you, and to scope them out in kind. Here's how to make the experience for the better.

Why Interview?

The risks that accompany having to strike a good impression in the flesh make it easy to bypass an optional interview. But there are a few reasons not to overlook the interview as your ally.

(1) Most interviews help. Unless your interview is an undeniable disaster (if they leave afraid of you, hating you, or nursing an open wound, you're not getting in), admissions review boards won't use the interview to scrap an applicant.

(2) It's easier to admit human beings than pieces of paper. Putting a face and a personality to your application gives your file a human touch.

(3) You can boost and reinforce your application. Even though the paperwork of an application might seem to go on forever, the actual amount of data that you put down barely sketches out who you are. Any chance you have to give the review committee another reason to admit you is a good thing.

Who Should Definitely Interview

Some people have a certain pizzazz that can't come across in an activities list. The interview is such a person's chance to show that they are more than a social security number. If you're likeable and

Don't get all up in the face of your interviewer! You'll get points docked if you don't stay out of his or her personal space, which for most Americans is between 30 and 36 inches.

Source:
www.collegegrad.com

leave a strong impression on people that you meet, then you should go out of your way to schedule an interview, even if it's inconvenient. The interview is also a golden opportunity to explain, one human being to another, the questionable parts of your application. You can make a case for the weak spots on your transcript that might cause a reviewer to hesitate in admissions. Outside circumstances, like personal issues, death in the family, even a learning disability, can be much more clearly explained and understood in the more personal atmosphere of the interview.

Tip: While the interview is a prime time to explain that pesky grade in woodshop ("You see, there's this disease called dowelphobia . . . "), you should be sure that you don't give off the image of an excuse-maker or a whiner. Your interview is not the time to cry on the shoulder of your new admissions friend. Remember that the admissions people seek those who face the winds of adversity and laugh, HA! If you can put a positive spin on your struggles, and use your explanation of the weakness to demonstrate strength, then you will not only justify any questionable sections of your application, but also show off what a great kid you are.

Who Should Think Twice

If you are horribly stop-breathing-when-other-people-talk-to-me shy, then you might want to think twice about the interview. People with crippling speech impediments or who are uncomfortable with English might also want to reconsider interviewing. But this applies to the most extreme cases. Remember that the interviewer is not an investigator waiting to fish out some weakness to wave to the admissions committees. Even if you are shy or you spit a lot when you talk, what you say, your confidence, and your enthusiasm matter more than the wet way in which you say it.

On- vs. Off-Campus Interview

On-Campus Interview

As the name suggests, this kind of interview takes place on campus, usually at the office of undergraduate admissions. When you make your whirlwind tour of college campuses, you'll get the most out of it if you go when school's in session. But if visiting twice is an option, you might want to schedule your interview during the summer. During the summer, schedules clear up and that means a more leisurely setting and a better chance to stand out and make an impression—just check to be sure that some permanent faculty will be around at your interview time. This ensures an interviewer who has some experience and who will be able to answer any questions that you might have. Also, you might not want to schedule the interview at the school of your dreams as your first interview. Having a few rounds of practice at some of your safety schools will help build up your confidence and familiarize you with the procedure.

Off-Campus Interview

The off-campus interview comes in a variety of shapes and sizes. Usually a local alumnus/a will conduct it. You might arrange to meet at your interviewer's house, at a local cafe, at her office, or in a restaurant. Usually your interviewer will contact you to set up a meeting time.

Who Interviews?

So who are these kooky people? Here's a breakdown of the three types of people who will be asking the questions.

Admissions Officer

PROS: The admissions officer interviews like it's his job. Mostly because it is his job. The most predictable of all the interviews, you can expect to find someone who is professional, and will direct the interview efficiently and attentively. With the admissions officer, the odds of encountering odd admissions shenanigans or pointless lines of questioning are much lower. It's also less likely that you'll have awkward silences or pauses with a person with as much interview know-how as the admissions officer. And as experienced recruiters, admissions officers can spout out all kinds of fun factoids to inform your opinion on the school.

CONS: Because the procedure is more cut-and-dry, the admissions officer's interview tends to resemble a job interview more than a conversation. Their knowledge of the school reflects the information you'll find in most thorough guidebooks as opposed to behind-the-scenes anecdotes and unofficial tidbits from students or alumni. In some cases, the admissions officer might not have even attended the school. So if you're looking forward to getting the dirt on the social scene and the best dorms on campus, the admissions officer might not be the best resource.

TO PREPARE: If you're interviewing after applying, remember that the admissions officer will likely be familiar with your file. Be ready to elaborate on any section of your application, and realize that many of the questions will be about specific items you've listed. (Time to explain how you managed to spend a total of 199 hours on activities in one week!)

Alumni Interviewer

PROS: These interviewers are just normal folks. The setting tends to be more relaxed and the pacing more casual. Think more Barbara Walters and less Chris Matthews. You can manage the direction and the pace of the interview more with alumni than

"People might tell you that if you're nervous, imagine your interviewer naked. Don't do this if your interviewer is really gross looking though!"

—Freshman, Yale University

with admissions officers, and the interviews tend to run a bit longer. The vast majority of alumni interviewers are good-natured people who just want to help out their alma mater and its prospective students (hey, could be you!).

CONS: These interviewers are just normal folks. Some might be socially inept, demanding, or not savvy to what it takes to write a powerful recommendation. Also, alumni interviewers won't necessarily be able to paint the most accurate picture of college life for your inquiring mind. Some have been away from campus for a long time and others just won't know that much about the details of the school.

TO PREPARE: Some colleges provide alumni interviewers with at least portions of your background information. But just in case, you might want to tow along your transcript and your resume. Definitely review all of your application materials ahead of time, and feel free to ask the interviewer at the beginning how much dirt on you the admissions office dished out. If it won't turn into a hassle, consider bringing along tapes of musical achievement, a copy of the school newspaper you edited, slides of artwork, pictures from your school play, or anything else that your mom would whip out to show off for company. Don't go overboard—a PowerPoint presentation on "The Wonder of Me" will look like you're trying too hard. Avoid anything that would involve dimming the lights, a tripod, or a laser pointer. Your objective is not a hard sell but a friendly conversation about your passions.

Student Interviewer

PROS: A handful of schools have started using current, enrolled students to conduct interviews. Not only will this help you get a better feel for the personality of the school, but your interviewer can be a great way to find out about actual student life. External stuff, like what you wear and your manners, will usually matter less to a student.

CONS: Most of us haven't had to sell ourselves to a peer, or even a near-peer! Don't be timid about talking about your achievements, but at the same time constantly monitor your tone to make sure that it would appeal to someone like you. Furthermore, the majority of students haven't had an opportunity to evaluate their peers. Student interviewers may not have the maturity or skills to navigate a fair interview.

TO PREPARE: Again, bring your transcript or résumé and be prepared to engage in conversations on any topic. Hedge against potential incompetence by having a set of safe topics to talk about in case you feel like the interview isn't moving forward.

Above all

Remember that no one species of interviewer is deadly. Most truly enjoy the chance to interact with prospective students, they like the people they meet, and most want to give them their best shot at admittance. Go in feeling good about your interviewer, and you'll likely leave the interview wearing the smile that you forced on the way in.

The Attitude They're Looking For

You can't puzzle together a model that will please all interviewers. But no matter what the school, no matter what the reputation, no matter who the interviewer is, there's one characteristic that repels all interviewers—acting unnatural. Even the densest interviewer will sniff out a poseur. Throwing in fancy SAT words that you don't understand ("My life philosophy is as ambidextrous as it is ostentatious") will not score you any points with your interviewer (or anyone else for that matter). Flinging your arms like you're being attacked by wild birds because you heard that gesturing was an important element to persuasive speech will only convince your interviewer that you're being attacked by wild birds. You are an excellent applicant. Don't distract from that or make them question your qualifications.

Dress: Think of the Interviewer as Your Grandma

Fortune may toss a blind midget named Antonio in your path, but to prepare for the interview, think grandma. When you're getting ready you should aim for the dress, manner, and attitude that would make your grandma pat you on the head, lean over to the person next to her and whisper, "What a nice young lady!" That is, unless you're a guy. But regardless, aim for the pat on the head. Your grandma would probably not pull out the pat for a guy sporting low-riding, torn-up jeans that reveal a pair of dirty boxers. That is, unless your grandma is Sisqó. On the other hand, putting on a three-piece suit and monocle screams "pretentious and unnatural!" into poor granny's ear. Look nice. Be comfortable. If you want to show off your personal style, that's wonderful, as long as it won't distract the interviewer and as long as it wouldn't offend any self-respecting grandmother.

Manners: Look Alive, Sonny!

Not only should you demonstrate what an upstanding, mature, and respectful citizen you are, you should also relay that you are an upstanding, mature, and respectful citizen through good manners. (They'll know you're sexy just by looking, so no need to convey that through the handshake or the smile, you sly devil, you!) On the other hand, being too cold and formal can turn an interviewer off—an upstanding person doesn't have to be aloof, or worse yet, robotic. Your goal should be to show that you're mature while not acting like a stiff. A big part of why many colleges interview is just to make sure that you aren't all bark and no bite. Balance maturity with confidence, energy with enthusiasm, and your interview will be a breeze! (That, and you'll make a great talk-show host if your veterinarian plan falls through.)

Tips for a Good Inverview
Start off with a firm handshake.
Sit up straight, and show that your interviewer is engaging you. Slouching and playing with your clothes, jewelry, or your pet chihuahua suggest boredom. (Note, you shouldn't bring your pet chihuahua.)
Smile.
Mind your pleases and thank yous.
Respect his or her space, and don't be afraid to occupy your own. Especially if the interview is in a personal area, like a home, be conscious of what you do. Don't put your feet on the furniture or snoop around. At the same time you shouldn't shrink into a little cocoon of timidity. Just remember to act as though you were in a bank—you wouldn't trample the furniture, but you also wouldn't act as though it would bite you.

Preparation

Besides going over your grade reports and activities lists, you should practice interviewing with family or friends. Have them ask you a couple of general interviewish questions and get used to being in the hot seat. If you feel weird about asking your family or your buddies to ask you about your academic mojo, practice in front of a mirror or with a video camera. Your goal is to excise all the stumbling and uncertainty before you go in. Pick out any habits that suggest nervousness ahead of time.

A good way to boost your confidence is to go in with a set of safe topics to talk about. For example, talking about the school never hurts and is easy to prepare for. Read any information that you can get about the college. Admissions packets and websites are good bets. Plus, if you visited the campus prior to your interview, think back on any memorable campus experiences. Was there a class that you visited that you can talk about? Conversations with students can be great springboards for questions and comments. For example, if the interview lags, you can bring up a conversation you had with a student about her research project on houseflies and horse dung. You can use this to discuss your own interest in research, to ask about student projects, or just to thrill in being able to incorporate the word "dung" into your discussion. Convince your interviewer of your passion for the school by knowing something about it. On the other hand, knowing nothing about it will only convince your interviewer that you haven't thought very carefully about college.

Other safe topics include any special areas of expertise that you have. If you know everything about car racing and have the enthusiasm of a stock-car driver, bring that up. These little areas of enthusiasm and expertise will make you seem like a good conversationalist, which is a great thing to be. They also serve to prevent awkward silences.

. . .

. . .

. . .

. . .

Be sure to maintain
eye contact with
your interviewer at
all times. After all,
it only takes six
muscles.

See, wasn't that weird? You should have something to pitch into the void to keep a comfortable air to the interview. You can always use the "one of the . . ." approach. Let's say the conversation stalls, start things up by saying something along the lines of "one of the things that appeals to me most about this school is . . ." or "one of my most memorable high school experiences was . . ." or "speaking of extracurriculars, one of my favorites was . . ." You don't want to get stuck talking about the weather or commenting on the décor of the office.

Some college counselors recommend flipping through magazines in order to get current information fast before you go in. While it doesn't hurt to familiarize yourself with current events before heading off into interviewland, avoid talking in detail about unfamiliar subjects. If you try and show what a worldly fella you are

by bringing up the article on the IMF that you glanced at over breakfast, you might find yourself in a cold sweat as your interviewer, the leading expert on international economics, wants to know your opinion about what's happening in Djibouti. If you find yourself helplessly facing down an interviewer who wants to quiz you with specific questions, try to turn the interview to subjects where you can demonstrate knowledge. Be honest. It's better to say "I don't know that much about Djibouti" than to try to fake or shake Djibouti. But don't just let unfamiliarity hang in the air like a black cloud of ignorance. Follow that up with something that shows that you still are a bright kid with plenty of non-Djibouti interests. "I'm more interested in the human rights aspect of international politics. That's why I started a letter writing campaign my sophomore year . . ."

"They can be kind of intimidating, but just know that even if you feel like you blew it, you're probably fine."

—Senior, Georgetown University

"Be sure to go to the bathroom before your interview! I didn't and I felt uncomfortable the whole time."

—Sophomore, Brown University

Some Sample Questions

Here are some questions that you should, without fail, know the answers to before you go into an interview:

Why do you want to attend this college? (As opposed to any other college?)

What do you want to do with your degree? (Nothing set in stone, they just want to make sure you've thought about a future beyond college.)

What are your greatest strengths/weaknesses?

Who are your major influences?

Those are just the basics. Be sure to ask friends, teachers, even parents for sample questions so that you have a good stock of answers ready for your interview.

The Rules

AIR QUOTES. Bad idea. Speak naturally.

SPECIFICS. The more specific you can be in your responses, the better. If your interviewer wants to know what your favorite class was in high school, don't just leave your answer at "physics." Talk about why you loved your physics teacher who had huge hair and would sing out equations, or the lab experiment where you chucked eggs over the football field to learn about gravity. Just as with the essay, you want to show, not tell. Paint a picture for your interviewer and you will be memorable and convincing.

THE LONG AND THE SHORT OF IT. You want to balance on the one hand stuffing your responses with yummy information and on the other hand being a babbling baboon. Vary the lengths of your responses. Don't make every answer an impassioned speech. Punch things up with some short, sweet, and specific responses to add snap to the conversation.

DOGS AND BEES CAN SMELL FEAR, but admissions officers can't. If you worry too much about the interview, you might come off as a nervous kid, but even then you're not doomed. Your interview is just one piece of the admissions puzzle, and your interviewer doesn't have enough weight to crush you in your tracks just because he doesn't like the color of your sweater. Relax and be confident!

THREE CHEERS FOR ENTHUSIASM. Don't let the formality of an interview dampen your friendliness or your energy. Even if your interviewer has as much life as Kirk Cameron's career, don't let that sap your vitality.

QUESTIONS. Ask them! Not only does this show interest but it also ensures that the conversation is more of a dialogue.

GRAMMAR. Look out for sounding clueless. Watch out for lots of "likes" and "you knows," and try to use pronouns and adverbs correctly.

Despite what we've written above, there are no fixed rules. These are all just suggestions—flexibility is your greatest friend. Listen more to the immediate demands of the interview than to what

Wearing a necktie to your interview? You might be interested to know that the modern necktie was made in the middle of the nineteenth century, during the Industrial Revolution.

we, or your Great Aunt Sally, tell you. If you try and force the session to fit your own agenda, or if you cram your interview into what you understand to be the "right" or "best" way to impress a person, you just end up coming off as unnatural and miss the opportunity to connect with a cool person from your potential college.

The Perfect Thank You

Although any conversation with a delightful applicant like yourself is a reward in itself, you should still thank the interviewer for the interview. Don't wait too long—while the image of your smiling face still burns bright in the interviewer's mind, sear your shining personality into his soul with a note thanking him for taking the time to talk to you. The formality of the note, which is conveyed in the tone and the all-important stationary decisions, should reflect the formality of the interview. Modify the tone and style of the note to fit your sense of the interview itself. If it was a cut-and-dry, job-type interview, a typed note might be more appropriate than a handmade card with ribbons, pressed flowers, and a puppy. For more intimate interviews, a handwritten card with a more personal voice could cement the initial interview connection. Regardless of your approach, there are a few key things to remember:

(1) A basic expression of gratitude for the interviewer's time and help.

(2) Something to show that you're interested and excited about the school (a few enthusiastic words about classes, or the sports team, or the campus are always good bets).

Don't arrive late to your interview! To make sure your watch is correct, set it against the atomic clock at the U.S. Naval Observatory, which is the official source of time for the United States Military.

Source: www.time.gov

"When my inter-
viewer asked me
what my favorite
book is, I told her
"War and Peace," so
I would look smart. I
hadn't read the book
though, so when she
asked me what my
favorite part was, I
looked really stupid."
—Junior, New York
University

(3) A specific reference to something you discussed in the interview. Just by referring to something you talked about will make you more memorable, and this can easily tie in with expressing interest in the school. If you're a drama buff, for example, mention what a pleasure it was getting more information about the fantastic theater program.

(4) Keep the note short and sweet. A handful of sentences is all it really takes.

CHAPTER EIGHT

Financing College

Going to college can demand more dough than a bakery in the land of the truly jumbo. But before you rip your liver out for sale on the black market, remember that (a) financial aid is out there and (b) you'll need that liver for when you start drinking alcohol. Whatever you do, don't dismiss a college for financial reasons or assume that you don't qualify for help. Some types of aid may appeal to you more than others—hint, it's a lot nicer to get money without dealing with paying it back—but while there's no guarantee of success, anything is worth a shot. So, ask! You may not receive, but there are some surprising (and not so surprising, i.e. work) ways to chisel down your debt.

Where Does the Financial Aid Package Come From?

(You See When Two Government Forms Love Each Other Very Much) . . . Behind the Scenes at the Financial Aid Office!!

The financial aid office may seem like some far away land where mischievous little elves toil over facts and figures and, with a few shakes of fairy dust, hand you a glittering sack of cash. So you may be asking yourself, "Who are these magical sprites and how can I get them to give me lots and lots of money?" Well, calculating a financial aid package is actually a lot more straightforward and requires far less fairy dust than you might imagine. Schools take the cost of attendance, subtract the amount of money your family can afford to pay, and presto! They arrive at your family's need.

Most books take this point as an opportunity to use a handy-dandy graphic to illustrate this complex equation. Are you ready for this? It goes something like:

College cost - Expected Family Contribution = Need

But how do they figure out how much college costs? The financial aid office takes certain costs of college as given. Tuition, fees, room, and board make up one section of cost. They also, however, take into account the expenses that will vary according to spending habits; many consider the money you'll have to fork over for books and supplies, your computer, transportation, and personal expenses. Keep in mind that some places skimp on the variable costs while others are more generous.

About that expected family contribution: Applying for aid means submitting the Free Application for Federal Student Aid (FAFSA) no matter where you want to go. Not only is this form the basis of your aid package, it's also fun to say. Using the Federal Methodology (the standards set by Congress), Uncle Sam will use your FAFSA to chug out your expected family contribution (EFC) and send it to you and your college choices in the form of the Student Aid Report. On top of the FAFSA many private schools require the CSS Profile and some ask for even more paperwork.

While the methodology that a financial aid office uses depends on the school, in general they weigh four factors:

(1) Parents' available income

(2) Parents' available assets

(3) Students' available income

(4) Students' available assets

Other stuff, like the number of people living in your house and the age of your parents, plays into the calculation of income. Assets include cash, savings and checking accounts, real estate, businesses and farms, investments, and (for schools that depart from the Federal Methodology) home equity. To get a better picture of what your expected family contribution will wind up being, try some of the online calculators. The websites www.finaid.org and www.collegeboard.org both will figure out your EFC for you. Not only does this reveal a better picture of whether your wallet should expect complete destruction or a gentle beating, it can also help you anticipate changes in your circumstances and strategize how to maximize your eligibility. Plus, visiting these websites can help fill any lonely Friday night—after all who needs friends when you've got asset protection? But don't forget that all of the planning and predicting that you can do shouldn't dictate where you apply, and you shouldn't assume your estimates are foolproof. Until you tear into that thick, juicy envelope, you really can't know for sure what your aid package will look like. Instead, use the ways of predicting aid as a good way to prepare for payment, not as a way to choose or rank schools. Leave that up to the elves.

Visiting the Office Itself

When you're on your whirlwind tour of college campuses, between shuffling after tour-guides and trying not to look like a visitor (even though your mom is taking "just one" picture of you with a water fountain), swing by the financial aid office. Just because they're called officers doesn't make them scary. So what should you ask when you're face-to-face with the man with the financial plan?

Good to Know

Guaranteed aid policy Do you guarantee to meet all of my need?

Costs What's the total cost of attendance? What other expenses await me?

Implementation Forget the amount of aid—how do you figure out what types of aid, and in what combinations, make up the package?

Policy on merit-based awards Will you look at my scholarships as part of the aid package or the family contribution when determining my need?

Methodology Will you throw in home equity when calculating need?

Good to Know

Need blind vs. need conscious Does applying for financial aid affect my chances of getting in?

Future aid How do you treat upperclass students? (in other words, are you going to lure me in with a sweet freshman package, and as I get old and grizzled, reduce my aid and leave me for a fresh, tight-bunned National Merit scholar?)

Merit-based scholarships You got 'em?

For non-need based options Will future grants or scholarships depend upon academic or extracurricular performance?

Loans Can I borrow more than you've offered me?

Summer earnings Did I serve hot dogs for this? What percentage of summer earnings will you expect from me?

The bottom-line What's it going to cost? How many loans will I need? How much average debt do students graduate with?

The Wide and Wonderful World of Forms!

For the love of FAFSA!!! As the name (Free Application for Federal Student Aid) implies, the form is free. So no matter who you are, you should pick one up and fill one out! Every year this form will anchor your aid package, and yes, you do have to re-file each year. To make things even easier in this hectic modern age, the form is also available online. At www.fafsa.ed.gov you can fill out our friend FAFSA and even sign the sucker electronically using a PIN. Doing this has several benefits:

A poll of U.S. under-graduate and graduate students found that 48 percent have bounced a check during college, 71 percent carry a credit-card balance, and 72 percent have called home for money.

Source:
www.cardweb.com

(1) Speed—if you file electronically, you can shave off 1-2 weeks from your processing time.

(2) Auto-edit—the online program will check your entries for you as you go along, so if you make a mistake, the program will let you know and smack you around a little (we made that last part up).

(3) EFC—FAFSA online will print out your EFC for you when you submit the data

(4) Corrections—you can go back and make corrections online; paper filers need to contact the Federal Student Aid Information Center to make any changes

(5) Environment—Heck, save a few trees.

You can also use the website to check the status of your application. If you don't have access to the Internet at home, remember that you can use the computers at schools and in public libraries. If you can't locate a computer and/or want to rage against the technology machine, you can get a hard copy of the form at your high school, financial aid offices, local libraries, or by calling the Federal Student Aid Information Center, 1-800-4-FED-AID.

Getting Started

Before you sit down and start trucking away with your bad financial aid self, you'll need some basic paperwork. Grab the following:

Social Security card

Driver's license

Alien Registration Receipt Card (if you're an alien)

W-2 Forms, Income tax returns, and 1099s for the previous year (yours and your parents')

Records of investments (stocks, mutual funds, etc.)

Records of untaxed income (Social Security, welfare, etc.)

Bank statements

Mortgage information

Records of child support

Business and farm records

Records of student grant, scholarship, and fellowship aid

Title IV Institution Codes (to have the government send the report to your schools, access these codes either online, by calling up your schools, or at your high school)

With these records, you should be set to fill out the forms.

It might sound a little over-the-top, but send those aid forms registered mail! A 1988 Postal Inspection Service study found that 76 percent of the post offices it checked up on had thrown away letters with paid postage. One current estimate has the U.S. Post Office throwing away upwards of a billion letters a week.

Words to the Wise

Make copies of everything and file them. As with everything for your college application, it never hurts to keep records. Plus, one-third of the FAFSAs that schools receive are selected for verification, meaning that they'll want to see all of your paperwork.

Keep deadlines in mind. Take care of business early. You can't submit before the first of January (they'll toss out all forms that come in early) but you should turn your form in as soon as possible after the first of the year. Getting your paperwork in early might qualify you for more dough at certain places and you'll be sure not to miss the different deadlines set by states, campus-based programs, etc. Christmas break is a good time to take care of all the forms, so break out the Yule, snuggle up with your 1040, and avoid the procrastination demons.

CSS Profile

If you're applying to a private school, chances are they'll want to know more about you before digging into their own pockets. You do have to pay to file as opposed to the FAFSA, but that five dollars (plus fifteen per school) is worth it given the aid you'll open yourself up to. Register by phone or at www.collegeboard.org to receive the profile, and remember that you can submit it in the fall.

Putting Your Poorest Foot Forward

Strategies to Get the Most Buck for Your Bang

You should not, under any circumstances at all, lie on the FAFSA or PROFILE. It's wrong, and you'll probably get caught, which would stink. There are, however, safe, ethical, and legal (wahoo!) ways to minimize your EFC, which will bump up your need at most schools. Your EFC reflects your family's financial situation based on standards that shelter certain funds and take into account family factors. By planning ahead, you can tailor your financial habits to whittle down that EFC. The factors that you can play with are income, assets, debt, household size, the number of family members enrolled in college, and dependency.

In a nutshell, you want to focus on decreasing income for the base year, sheltering assets that would otherwise be considered, maximizing household size and the number of family members also getting an education, and timing your independence with your filing. There are many ways to do all this, but some are more reasonable than others. For example, dependency changes if you're married before you submit, but hitting the mail-order bride catalogs might be a bit hasty. Also, remember that increasing your aid package doesn't always make the best financial sense in the big picture. Always do what is in your best interest in the long run. Here are a few of the simplest ways to make sure that you are the right amount of needy at the right time.

(1) LOWER YOUR PARENTS' INCOME: Keep capital gains low by selling stocks early. Have your parents sell any stocks that they were planning to use for college before January of your junior year, which keeps the capital gain separate from your family's income during the financial aid year. Likewise, the interest payment from cashing savings bonds can pump up income—cash those puppies in early or wait until after your FAFSA years have passed.

(2) KEEP YOUR ASSETS LOW: Save in your parents' names. While the tax rate for your income is lower, for financial aid, the chunk of your money that you're expected to contribute (35%) is a whole lot higher than your parents' expected income contribution (5%). Save your money in your parents' names and the amount you're expected to pony up goes down.

(3) SHIFT ASSETS: If you already have a bunch of money saved up, spend it before you dip into mom and dad's piggybank. If you have expenses that are for your benefit (like summer camp or private high school tuition), pay for them out of your account. When you stock up for college, make sure your assets are footing the bill for your computer, car, or deluxe Microfridge 2000.

(4) POSTPONE GIFT MONEY: So grandma finally wants to give you something better than long underwear—a nice fat savings bond for her little college man. Resist temptation, friend! Have her either wait until you graduate and use the money to pay off your loans, ask her give it to your parents, or look into whether your school allows grandparents to make direct payments to it.

(5) REDUCE YOUR PARENTS' ASSETS: Buy big before you file. If your family will be making big purchases, you might as well make them during the year that counts for aid, which will lower liquid assets. Don't have your folks make purchases just to shed assets (note—buying an elephant to manipulate your aid package won't pay off), but it's a good idea to time necessary big-ticket expenses with filing.

(6) RETIREMENT FUNDS, TAX DEFERRED ANNUITIES, AND LIFE INSURANCE POLICIES, OH MY! FAFSA and CSS don't consider things like retirement funds as assets, so your parents should maximize their contributions to their IRA's before January of your junior year. Likewise, it doesn't make sense for your parents to use money from their retirement accounts to pay for school.

(7) HAVE YOUR FAMILY HIT THE BOOKS: If your parents or other family members are getting 6+ college credits, this can knock off a big chunk from your EFC. A little bit of book learnin' in night school not only can teach your mom C++, but it can get you extra aid.

In 1987, University of Illinois freshman Mike Hayes launched a brilliant campaign to finance his education. He had a request published in the *Chicago Tribune* that asked strangers to send him one penny each. Since the column reached so many people around the country, and thanks to an overwhelming response, Hayes was able to rake in the $28,000 he needed.

(8) LOANS—BUH-BYE DEBT!
The Feds don't take consumer debt or home equity into account. So if you pay off things like your credit card, pre-pay your mortgage, and minimize educational debt, you can increase your aid eligibility. Neat, huh?

Why is Stafford Lending Me Money When I'm Going to Harvard?

For the vast majority of us, "financial management" has meant foraging in the couch cushions for enough change to buy a Slurpee. Well prepare to change your life! After reading this section, you'll understand the actual components of your aid package. No more awkward pauses in cocktail party conversations about Pell Grants. No more embarrassing "I don't understand accrual" body odor. While not always super-thrilling, being able to dissect and assess your package grants you independence and prevents any rude financial awakenings down the road. So before you hand this book over to your folks, you should know that while tons of parents mind the financial gate of their kids, *your* aid determines the debt that *you* may be responsible for paying back after *you* graduate. Being involved in your aid process from FAFSA to shining FAFSA will pay off. So grab that Slurpee and prepare for the financial ride of your life.

Types of Aid

Grants

Grants are financial aid that you don't need to repay. They come in two basic flavors, Pell Grants and Federal Supplemental Educational Opportunity Grants. For the 2000–2001 academic year Pell Grants ranged from $400–3300, while the FSEOG ranged from $100–4000. Using your FAFSA, and with the wave of a Congressional formula, the federal government figures out your Pell Grant award. The funding changes from year to year based on the mood of Congress, but if you apply on time and qualify, you'll get your dough. On the other hand, FSEOG grants are campus-based, meaning that the schools administer disbursement. The funding varies depending on the school (some schools don't participate at all), and because the money has a cap—unlike the Pell Grant—the earlier you apply the better your odds of getting aid are.

Some good news . . . as of this printing, President Bush was planning to up the amount of Pell Grant aid that freshmen receive by 50 percent. He was also planning to tack $1000 in aid for Pell Grantees who took advanced math and science classes in high school.

And now, some not-so-good news . . .

Loans

Today, loans make up a huge piece of the financial aid pie. Since 1980, loans increased from 41 to 59 percent of aid packages. That means that, along with a mastery of Playstation, the average student leaves college with $15,000–$20,000 in debt.

The Lingo

It's important to be able to talk the loan talk when you walk the financial aid walk. Here are a few financial terms that will help you talk to the financial aid office. Plus, you can earn huge brownie points if you toss one of these puppies out at the dinner table.

accrued interest The accumulated interest charged on the principal of a loan

borrower (a.k.a. maker) The person that "loan shark Guido" will come after in case of default. It's the person who signs the promissory note and therefore owns responsibility for repayment.

capitalized interest During repayment, this is your accrued interest plus the amount of principal that you still need to repay.

consolidation A way to simplify repayment and possibly lock in a lower interest rate, consolidation lets you combine your loans into one bright and shiny new loan.

default Avoid this at all costs! Default is failure to repay according to the terms agreed to on the promissory note. If you default, you wreck your credit record, you might ruin your eligibility for new federal aid if you go back to school, and you endanger your paycheck and tax refund.

deferment Putting off payment. This is allowed under many circumstances, such as enrollment in graduate school.

disclosure statement A statement that outlines your repayment plan. You have a right to this before you start repayment.

fixed interest rate An interest rate that doesn't change over the period of a loan

forbearance During times of personal financial woe, the government sometimes cuts you some slack on repayment by postponing or reducing your loan payments.

grace period The breathing space you receive for six to nine months after graduation (or less than half-time enrollment) before you have to start writing those checks. It's like the honeymoon from a *really* expensive wedding.

guaranty agency The administrator of the FFEL at your school.

origination fee The money up front that you have to pay for certain loans, such as the Stafford.

promissory note The contract that details the terms of the loan and repayment. This sucker is legally binding and will come back to haunt you if you don't respect its terms.

prepayment Your right to start digging into your debt before it's due.

secondary market In order to get more money to lend, banks will sell their loans to the secondary market.

variable interest rate An interest rate that changes over time, generally according to the Treasury Bills or the Prime Rate.

Stafford

Participating schools employ either the Direct Loan program or the Federal Family Education Loan. In terms of interest rates and deferment policies, the programs are identical. Both types offer a yearly variable interest rate capped at 8.25 percent. In the end you'll have a ten-year repayment schedule and a $50 minimum monthly payment. The difference between the two is the source of the money—with Direct Loans the government gives you the money through the schools. On the other hand, an FFEL will come from a private lender (banks, credit unions). What you get depends on the school you go to.

The difference between the two means that if you get an FFEL loan, you'll need to do some lender-hunting. Since most places offer just about the same interest rates and terms, you shouldn't agonize over your choice, but it doesn't hurt to look for a couple of characteristics that ease the ouch of repayment.

Using a bank that sells its loans on the secondary market to either Sallie Mae (the Student Loan Marketing Association) or USA Group will keep your future interest payments down. Both organizations have incentives for on-time repayment that mean savings for you. Check out www.salliemae.com and www.usagroup.com.

The frequency of capitalization can affect the amount of interest you pay for unsubsidized loans. Look for a lender that capitalizes only once when the loan goes into repayment to avoid paying interest on interest.

Repayment options such as consolidation and graduated repayment can let you access the best possible rates and terms.

Remember that service matters. In order to make paying off your debt as convenient and painless as possible, find one lender you like and stick with it through college. Your financial aid officer and state guaranty agency can work some matchmaking magic to help you find a compatible lender. (Check out your blue pages for state guaranty agency listings).

When life hands you lemons, sometimes you have to defer repayment on the lemonade stand. Different lenders have different forbearance policies. Look for one that's flexible.

Subsidized and unsubsidized

Stafford loans can be subsidized or unsubsidized. With subsidized loans, during your enrollment,

The National Organization for the Reform of Marijuana Laws (NORML) gives out scholarships in recognition of achievement in their annual essay contest in which students propose more "sensible" drug policies for the United States.

Source: www.norml.org

good ol' Uncle Sam will handle your interest payments. He'll continue to help you out for six months after graduation and during any deferment period. You shouldn't pass up the opportunity to get four years of interest-free borrowing. On the other hand, with unsubsidized loans, which are not based on need, the meter starts as soon as you borrow. There are deferment options, but you should compare the interest rates of unsubsidized loans to other lenders. While you won't find a better deal than a subsidized loan, other borrowing sources, like home equity loans, will sometimes outperform an unsubsidized loan.

Perkins Loans

Another federally funded program, Perkins Loans, use the school to administrate federal funds at a rock-bottom interest rate of 5 percent. Most of the money goes to extremely needy full-time students, and the amount of money available depends on the school.

In the case of Perkins loans, choice of career can influence your loan repayment. So don't get too scared off by the prospect of debt if you plan to devote yourself to a life without material trappings. Perkins loans make exceptions for certain professions (such as teaching) that can result in loan cancellation.

PLUS

So far, the loans we've talked about lend to students, but for families that still have unmet need, parents can borrow money using the non-need based Parent Loans for Undergraduate Students. Like Stafford loans, PLUS loans include two programs, Direct

PLUS Loans and Family Federal Education Loans. Similarly, the two have the same terms but different origination; Direct Loans come directly from the government, while the FFEL comes from a private lender. These loans require a credit check and have no annual borrowing limits (meaning that you should exercise some restraint and figure out what you can afford to repay before diving in).

Supplemental Loans

Still need money? You or your parents can try on a supplemental, or alternative, loan for size. Privately sponsored and insured, lenders won't require collateral but determine eligibility based on credit history. Although sometimes comparable to PLUS loan rates, usually these guys will hit you harder in terms of interest rates and fees. Don't forget that other loans like home equity may offer a more attractive plan.

Evaluating Your Loan

When assessing what kind of loan bundle you want to take with you, there are a few main things to consider:

interest rate What is it, how is it determined, and is it fixed or variable?

borrower Who's going to be responsible for payment, you or you folks?

repayment options These include term of repayment, time of repayment, and prepayment.

origination fees Are there any, and what are they?

cosigner Is one permitted or required?

tax deductibility Keep in mind that interest on certain loans (like home equity) is tax deductible. This can trim your payments.

Work-Study

So even with loans and grants up the financial wazoo, you still might have to roll up your sleeves and do some work to pay for college. Before you moan and groan about having to devote your youth to working for the man, and before your parents start stressing about the time you'll sap from your academics, remember that work-study can be incredibly flexible and that employment often educates you as much as your classes. By all means, search the databases that most schools have online and check out jobs galore on bulletin boards in the student employment office. But if you can't find anything more exciting than cleaning out toilets or standing guard at the library, keep in mind that non-profit work as well as work that's related to your field of study can count for funding, too. Staffing that soup kitchen and tutoring those kiddoes not only promise to put you on Santa's good list, but also can be sources of work-study aid. Talk to the good people at your student employment office to find out about the variety that's available, the hours you'll need to work, and the assignment of jobs. When you get in touch with them, find out about wages, application for jobs, and method of pay. Don't forget that you can customize your employment to your needs—understand your options.

Scholarships

In terms of costs and benefits, some argue that scholarship applications don't pay off considering the time you devote, the competitiveness of the applications that offer significant awards, and the fact that most schools slice your award money right out of your aid package, which means you still pay the same. And although everybody's mom seems to know (insert lame kid's name here) who's going to (prestigious college) "on a full scholarship!" the truth is that private scholarships make up less than 5 percent of total annual aid. Most students don't get private funds to finance college. But don't just write off scholarship applications as too much trouble and melt into a warm puddle of senior mush— mmm . . . senior mush. Winning a scholarship will never hurt you. Awards generally decrease college

On ways to budget effectively: American Airlines saved $40,000 in 1987 by eliminating one olive from each salad served in first-class.

costs, pad your résumé, and bring the glory of victory. So even if waves of motivation aren't exactly pounding at your shores—i.e. you think of yourself as mediocre or you just turn into a big lazy fart—you should still search for scholarships.

And more good news! A number of top private schools (like Princeton, Harvard, and other bow-tie-wearing colleges) opted to loosen the squeeze on middle-class and upper-middle-class families with policies that shift away from loans to grants, ease up on student contribution, and cap home equity as an asset. Now, many of the top dogs that don't offer merit-based aid pump up need-based aid by using scholarships that you win to reduce the amount of loans you have to pay off (instead of treating your winnings as an asset and sucking them away). Bottom line: find out how your prospective colleges treat your hard-earned scholarship dough. While you're at it, research which schools offer merit-based scholarships. Schools like Oberlin and Vanderbilt put more oomph into their financial aid plans with beefier merit-based scholarship allowances, offering mo' money to mo' types of students.

The Hunt

While there may not be enough money out there for everyone to get a scholarship, there certainly is enough variety for everyone to have a decent shot when applying. There are two basic forms of scholarships. One bases judgment on stuff you've done and who you are, and the other asks you to actively compete by writing an essay or performing a task. Often, you'll get a mix between the two types. So, to start your search, it helps to think about what distinguishes you from the crowd. You should consider three things: your background, your connections, and your interests. Ask yourself, "Self, who's yo' daddy?" If you are a part-Inuit, left-handed, son of a veteran, you can find a scholarship to apply for, or at least pinpoint an angle to work for more general applications. Work your connections; look into whether your parents' companies or clubs use scholarship programs. Here are a few more things to think about:

Heritage

Gender

Intended major

Career objective

Hobbies, sports, and activities

Memberships and associations

Religion

Disabilities

Talents

In terms of the actual search, tons of internet options are out there. The variety of search engines that claim to be the best and biggest along with the sheer quantity of scholarships that they can pull up for you can be a little daunting. We like www.fastweb.com—the listings are comprehensive and easy to sort through. What really makes the site great is that it does the

The average college student spends $900 a year on alcohol and $450 a year on books

Source:
www.factsontap.org

organizing for you, links you to scholarship websites, offers email deadline notification, and facilitates online applying. But shop around on several sites and see what interface you like best. Just don't get carried away by trying to continue accounts on a gazillion sites. An initial search on many different sites can give you an idea of the variety of scholarships out there and is an excellent way to start, but when you're maintaining your account, stick to only one or two databases in order to simplify organizing the scholarship information that they pull up for you. Trying to keep up accounts on every search engine out there might distract you from your viable options. Here are some other popular search sites:

www.finaid.org

www.fastaid.com

www.srnexpress.com

And venture beyond your computer! Poke around online, but remember that your college counseling office usually keeps tons of scholarship resources often in the form of pricey databases, and including local scholarships that you might have a better shot at. Talk to your favorite teachers, or at least the teachers of your favorite subjects, and dig out any competitions they may know of. Diligence pays off. Keep checking back with your contacts, scope out bulletin boards, and always be on the lookout for opportunities.

Applying

With the limitations on scholarships in mind, there are a few general rules to think about:

(1) Focus on securing other forms of aid first. Don't neglect your federal aid applications and deadlines in pursuit of a scholarship.

(2) Stay organized. File all your application materials, keep a calendar of deadlines, and create an application toolbox filled with recommendations, potential essays, and lists of awards and extracurriculars.

(3) Don't delay. Putting off applying for scholarships will not make the process easier.

Getting a scholarship takes more than a trip to Kinkos to copy off your college application. Even more so than your college application evaluators, scholarship judges seek specific qualities and compare you directly to your competition. Considering the higher level of comparison, make yourself stand out. This doesn't mean that you should use funky colors of paper or sparkles—unless you're applying for the funky-color-and-sparkles scholarship, in which case, glitter away! Rather, you should consider your most unique or strongest selling point and work that puppy to death. Target an image and cultivate it—you should build your application around a memorable theme. Whether it's superstar athlete, entrepreneur, or saintly community-service freak, a snapshot of a particularly strong part of your personality or past distinguishes you from the crowd at decision time. Also, don't be afraid to contact the sponsors themselves. A clearer picture of the person who's on the judging side of your application will make crafting your entry easier. If you're wondering what they're looking for in the application, call up and ask them, or even request samples of winning entries. When you get samples, look for what appeals to the judges and mold your application to that standard. We're not saying you should rehash the entry—originality always pays off. Instead, try and get a sense of the personality and preferences of the judges and apply accordingly.

AS A WORD OF CAUTION. You will likely run into advertisements for agencies that offer to find you great scholarships for a small fee. Our advice is to ignore all of these offers unless someone you know, and know well, recommends them to you specifically. There are a lot of scam artists out there who simply take your money and run, or just feed the information you give them into one of the many free finders on the web. They're devious, and they know how badly you need money, so they prey on that need. We're really hopeful that none of our readers will give them even a cent and they'll have to look into a more honest trade. Shame on you fake scholarship finders!

So, How Big Is YOUR Package?

Letter Number 2: The big day has finally come. You've torn into the thick envelope, kissed, cried, danced a little "I'm going to college, wahoo!" jig, and otherwise celebrated acceptance. In your jigging excitement, it can be easy to take the less thrilling task of dissecting your award letter lightly or to act hastily. The award letter is the handy-dandy document that arrives a few months after your early acceptance letter, or around the same time for a regular acceptance letter. It lays out all the components of your financial aid fun-bag and comes with a handful of documents that you sign to accept the offer. If you're like us, you get excited when somebody offers you a bright shiny quarter, so the number of zeros in the award letter can tempt you to sign, and to sign fast. But before you whip out your pen, you should sit down, preferably with your parents, and go over each package. When assessing award letters, here are a few things to keep in mind:

DON'T LOOK AT THE TOTAL AMOUNT OF AID. Consider how much your EFC is, not the amount of money they offer you. Remember that even though a pricey school may throw more money your way, the amount you wind up paying may still be more than a cheaper school that offers you a smaller package.

The New England Chapter of the National Association to Advance Fat Acceptance offers a $500 scholarship to overweight seniors attending high school in the New England area who are prepared to attend a two- or four-year university.

Source: www.home-stead.com/necnaafa

CONSIDER OUTSIDE COSTS. Will you need a car if you attend a certain college? How much is airfare going to cost you? What is the going rate of self-defense classes in New Haven?

SIZE CERTAINLY MATTERS. But how much? If there are significant differences in package sizes, it helps to measure the cost of the school against how much going to that particular school means to you. Try making a pros and cons list for your college choices.

FIGURE OUT AN IDEAL DISTRIBUTION OF AID. If work-study jobs don't appeal to you, or if one college is offering more grants than loans, that can make a huge difference between two otherwise identical packages.

Keep in mind that the award letter is not the end of the financial aid decision. Room to wiggle the amount and type of aid still exists.

A good way to organize your comparison is by grabbing a calculator and mapping out the expense of enrollment. Figure out the upfront costs for each of the schools—in other words, how much will you have to pay outright? Then, calculate how deep a debt-hole you dig at each college. Debt, as a general rule, sucks. It's terrible not to be able to pay your "automo-bills." So when you weigh your grant and loan distribution, use your pros and cons list for the colleges, and try to figure out how much owing money means to you.

Although you should exercise prudence before accepting a package, you shouldn't dilly-dally around too much either. Accepting an aid package does not equal a decision to attend that college. If a package looks good to you, avoid missing any deadlines by accepting it. You can notify the colleges later if you decide not to attend.

What's That Smell?

So you need to deal with a stinky aid package. Before you despair because that dream school carries a hefty price tag, remember that you still have some power. Contact your aid office in order to either notify them of extenuating circumstances or engage in a little bargaining. There are some dos and don'ts when it comes to wheeling and dealing with your package.

DON'T: Barge into the financial aid office in tears, brandishing a saber and declaring the financial aid officer a heartless scalawag.

DO: Set up an appointment (preferably face-to-face, or over the phone if distance is a factor). Go into the meeting with a list of problems with the package and questions about alternative payment. If there has been a change in circumstances make sure you have it all in writing when you bring it in (or fax it in). Your officer will want a hard copy of any mitigating circumstances. Above all, be professional; be clear; and be nice. It can only help you.

DON'T: Resign yourself to an unsatisfactory package.

DO: Remember that you can partially accept any given offer. No one will force you to accept a loan, and you aren't required to perform work-study. If you want to, you can be selective when it comes to your aid offer.

DON'T: Ignore your bargaining power.

DO: Roll up your sleeves and bring any significantly better offer to the attention of tight-fisted schools. Bargaining has its limitations—it usually works only with schools of comparable stature, it only applies to money that the colleges dish out from their own coffers, and it varies according to the college's desire to snag you for their student body. Nevertheless, don't be afraid to try and negotiate a better deal.

DON'T: Procrastinate.

DO: Contact your financial aid office right away with a clear outline of your problems. Generally, the earlier you get in touch with the financial aid office, the more flexible an officer will be when it comes to tweaking your package.

Pain in the Assets— Saving for College

Because assets can decrease a financial aid package, people assume that saving for college doesn't do any good. But the truth is that most colleges try not to penalize parents who prepare for Junior's education by setting some money aside. While the financial aid office hands out money to low-income families, it's not going to take pity on a high-earning, high-rolling family that fritters away money at The Sharper Image and expects the college to subsidize its collection of gas-operated, musical fingernail clippers. Savings pays off, and here are a few reasons why:

(1) The financial aid office respects parents who work to fund their kids' educations. Impress your financial aid officer—it never hurts when she crafts your package.

(2) You need to keep your options open. Banking on a particular college price tag, admissions policy, or expected aid is never a good idea in the wild and wacky world of financial aid. Savings will cushion any unexpected expenses or changes in heart that a kid might face.

(3) A huge chunk of the financial aid cookie is usually loans. This leaves you with a choice—saving in advance gives you the chance to earn interest on your piggybank, while needing to borrow when you go off to school will force you to pay interest later.

(4) While your holdings might decrease aid initially, any spending to cover freshman year will decrease assets for sophomore year, which will probably make you eligible for more aid then.

So even though it's not fun, it's smart to save.

College Choice

When you thumb through any listings of colleges, the sticker price can leap out and punch you in the nose. Don't let it. While at face value it's cheaper to spend the next four years going to Disneyland every day, the actual money you'll need to shell out depends upon the amount of aid they'll give you. Likewise, a college that may be a bargain on paper may not come through in the financial aid game as well as schools with bigger endowments. When you apply to schools, remember not to be averse to the diverse. You shouldn't box yourself into a financial hole by considering schools of just one type, region, or price range. At the same time, applying to a gazillion colleges just for the sake of variety wastes time, energy, and money. But keeping an open mind when it comes to choosing the colleges you apply to yields pleasant surprises and adds to your bargaining power in case you've got to haggle. For example, if you'd really like to go to college A but college B gave you a full ride, telling college A the scenario might just loosen their purse strings for you a little. If it doesn't, keep an open mind about that full ride—you'll appreciate it later in life if you have no loans to pay off to college A.

Community College vs. Four-Year

While you shouldn't let a scary price tag keep you from applying to the four-year colleges of your choice, keep in mind that community college educations offer a whole bag of benefits. Most community colleges are public, two-year schools that have open admissions—meaning that anyone can attend, and you don't need no stinkin' Scantrons to get in. Many people use them as a stepping stone, spending two years at a community college and going on to graduate from a four-year school. A big bonus is that they cost about half as much as a four-year public college (and you can cut costs even more if you live at home), and that savings isn't necessarily at the expense of the quality of your education. Often the faculty has the same fancy credentials as those at four-year colleges but without the research commitments that can limit

A 1999 study conducted by the U.S. Department of Education reports that 70 percent of two-year college graduates go on to also receive bachelor's degrees at other schools.

professor involvement at universities. Plus, studies show that graduates from four-year colleges who get their start at junior colleges have the same level of academic preparation as the kids who go straight to the four-year. Smaller classes that accommodate more schedules make things easier for students who have special needs, like work or family commitments. If you're seriously considering community colleges, it doesn't hurt to look into taking a night class or a summer-school class while you're in high school. Test out the waters and see if a two-year school might be the best deal in town.

So plan carefully, explore any options that come up, and keep an open mind. We wish you the best of luck, because trust us, you're gonna need it!

CHAPTER NINE

Hopping Ponds

Applying as a Transfer Student

For whatever reason, you might get to college and realize that you should have gone somewhere else. Well, there's just as much to know about transferring as there is to know about applying in the first place. As usual, we're here to help. The following chapter is our guide through transfer admissions, with advice and quotes from kids who actually made the leap . . . and are pretty happy with the results.

Preparing to Transfer

Just like applying to college, what you have done matters just as much as what you *are doing*. In other words, the first secret to transfer success is to make the most out of the time you're spending at your current school. Your new school won't care a bit about what a fabulous student you were in high school if you can't show them evidence that you kept it up into college. The problems you are having with your current school should have more to do with the school than with you. (Otherwise, why would another school work any better?) It helps your case immensely if you have good reasons for transferring.

Some reasons are better than others. Bad reasons would be if you've ticked off too many administrators at your current school or you don't think the undergraduates have a good enough party scene. Better reasons might be that the programs at your current school, no matter how hard you have worked in them, won't give you everything you need in your education. In order to show the people at your prospective school that the last statement applies to you, it's important to have a few things shine through from your experience at your previous college.

First off, have you been taking full advantage of the school you're at now? Colleges will want to know this, and they know that you'll just say "of course!" if asked, so they're a little keener about finding the answer. When they look through your transcript, they'll want to learn a few specific things. If you're applying to transfer to a liberal arts school, like Harvard, the admissions committee will be checking to see if you spread your academic interests out and looked at more than just your major's department for challenging courses. If, on the other hand, you are moving from a liberal arts education to a more specialized one, the prospective school will want to see that you've exhausted a great deal of your present school's resources in that area and have a need to really branch out in that field.

It probably goes without saying that if you're applying to a school that, for whatever reason, is considered a "better" school academically than the one you're at, you should only be taking the most challenging classes at your current school. If you weren't willing to challenge yourself at an easier school, why should they expect you to cut it at a harder institution? As a precautionary note, specialized pre-professional or technical classes might be challenging, fun, and worth your time, but to a liberal arts school, they might look like a lack of love for the liberal arts way, or they might not count towards your degree. This might leave your choice school wondering if you'd have time to finish your degree. If you are applying to a more liberal school and have some very specialized courses, you should let them know how you'd plan on finishing your degree on time, or let them know that you would pursue an extra semester or two to have time to finish.

Taking advantage of your present school means taking advantage of the courses you pick. You shouldn't be just getting by in a class because a good grade means a better recommendation.

"Before I even arrived [at Harvard], other transfer students contacted me, ensuring my transition would be as comfortable as possible."

—Transfer Student, Harvard University

Some schools let you apply to transfer using the common application, even though the questions are more geared towards high school students, and you might have used it to apply to your first school.

In your grades and letters from professors, your new school will see your performance at a college level, something they can't do with applications from high school students. Because the real gamble with accepting a student is whether or not they'll work out in a college environment, these indicators are big on the list of what will get you into your new school. You stand a great chance of getting in if another college had good things to say about your performance. Simple, right?

Other ways to take advantage of your school include clubs, teams, Greek life, and other activities. These things take on a few roles in the transfer application that they don't take in the application of high school students. Illustrating how you were able to participate in the college community shows a lot about your ability to handle your time wisely, and it makes you look more sociable, which is a bonus since they fear accepting shut-ins who hop schools to try out a better social scene. Don't be too drastic—you don't need that two-page activity list stapled on the back of your application like when you applied from high school. Just make sure that you account for your out-of-class time with some finesse. Even if you've only been involved in a few activities at college, it will make a difference. Showing commitment to a few things, as we've said in the high school chapter, doesn't make you seem lazy, it shows that you are dedicated. And, if one of those interests is something you've really shined at while in college, it will just add that much more to your desirability. You catch, you!

Selling Yourself . . . the Legal Way!

Now that you've got great grades in lots of the right classes, a pile of recommendations from all your favorite professors, and the application to your new school, it's time for the real beef of transfer admissions: selling yourself to another school. In every step of the process, you should try to sell a student who is bright, motivated, and who hasn't been fully challenged at his or her current school. Just keep thoughts like that in mind when you're filling in all those forms and writing new personal statements. It will color your application much better than if you fill everything in while thinking about how much you hate your English professor and how you can't wait to rub your acceptance letter in your roommate's face. Stuff like that comes

through, and nobody wants that kind of student, even if those are your only flaws—bad motivation for transfer is *the* deadly sin of transfer admissions.

The Application

You probably figured this out on your own, but it's *really* important to be on time with all of your application materials. If you're worried about anything getting lost, it's never a horrible idea to send things registered mail. (That's where they sign for it when they get it.) But do check to make sure that the prospective school's admissions office is cool with that. Most important, really, is just setting your own deadlines for stuff and following through. If you really want to transfer, now's the best time to show that you are a responsible, prompt, efficient person. So stop procrastinating and go to it!

In the course of applying, you'll need the following things sent to your prospective school(s):

(1) Transcripts from all schools attended since and including secondary school. This includes summer schools, community colleges, whatever. Make sure they all go out. Also, if there are rules regarding "official" and "non-official" grade reports, get those from the prospective schools *before* you send everything out.

(2) SAT score reports sent directly from ETS or College Board, even if they are listed on your college or high school transcript.

(3) A formal statement from the dean's office that you are in good academic and disciplinary standing at your current college or university.

(4) The full, completed application for the school to which you are applying. (Makes sense.) This includes a well-written essay, of course, that should talk more about you as a college student than you when you first applied to college or even earlier. In other words, make sure that you show something learned in your time at college, and don't, by any means, just use the essay you used for freshman admissions, unless it's damned near Pulitzer quality. You can also use the personal statement to show specifically why you are transferring, and justify your actions (including your academic performance if needed), at your current school. Once again the mantra: bad motivation is *the* deadly sin in transfer admissions.

(5) At least two letters of recommendation from *college* professors (high school teachers, friends of the family, etc. will not cut it, remember what we said about the new school seeing what you're like at *college*.) Make sure they are professors who know you well and had you in class recently to ensure the best application. Also, don't be shy about speaking up and telling the professor why you want a really great recommendation, as well as why you deserve it. But also remember to give professors everything they need to write a good recommendation: the form (if any), the envelope (stamped and addressed), copies of your work in his or her class, your résumé, and time!

Note: While most schools do not offer interviews for transfer applicants, if you have any chance for something like an interview (a visit to the admissions office, contact with the athletic department, etc.), take that opportunity to put a face and personality to your application for all it's worth. In case you didn't know, it's worth a lot!

Your Odds

If you really are applying to a school because it has a program that best meets your needs, you should only apply to schools with similar programs. You should always keep in mind that your motivation will come into question if a prospective school thinks you're transferring because you need a great astrophysics program, and then finds out you also applied to transfer to liberal-arts colleges that don't even have labs. Be consistent in your search.

That being said, schools that really do have great programs are also probably pretty selective, and if your current college isn't cutting it, you really ought to have other transfer options. You should make the most of your education, even if you can't transfer to, say, Harvard, who only takes 60 out of about 2,000 transfer applicants a year!

Athletic Transfers: Hopping Ponds for Highly Skilled Hoppers

If you are a competitive athlete, you might as well use your abilities to help further entice a new school. Once you've started applying, it's a good idea to write a letter or an email to coaches

"Transferring is essentially having to apply to college again, which is immensely daunting at the outset, but [Harvard] does a superb job at facilitating the process."

—Transfer Student, Harvard University

at prospective schools, letting them know about your athletic achievements, where else you're applying, and logistical stuff like SAT scores and your current GPA. You can still be recruited at this stage of the game, and if your numbers impress a coach, it can only help your chances of getting in.

If you are or were competing at your current school, especially if you signed with that school for any type of athletic scholarship, you'll need to get an NCAA athletic release form from your current school's NCAA compliance director before you can be recruited by the new school. It's also important to consider that you must complete a full year at the first institution with which you signed, or else you must forfeit (sit out from competition) at your new school for a year (if for instance, you transferred after only your first semester at your current school).

If you really hope to keep competing, better play by the NCAA's rules!

Getting In and Going

Once you successfully transfer, and we hope you do if that's what you're after, there are a lot of challenges to face that you should be aware of before heading out. For one, meeting people at your new school might be a little challenging, since everyone else has been developing friendships since freshman week. The best advice we can give you is to get out there and get involved with your new school's community. Not too much, now—you don't want to sink under the social weight of ten new clubs—but it will really help build friends and a love of your someday alma mater.

The other big piece of advice we can offer is to live on campus.

"The school I went to was too small for my tastes; its hard to know what kind of school you want before you go there."

—Transfer Student, Harvard University

Living on campus helps put you in the center of college life, and guarantees at least a few people you'll get to know right away at your school. These kinds of instant contacts will really pay off around course-selection time, and they might just be your friends for life. Who could deny themselves a better opportunity to meet people like that? So if there's any way you can squeeze yourself into the dorms at your new college, it will make the transition all that much better.

CHAPTER TEN

International Applicants

So you want to go to school in America—that idyllic land of the free and the brave, the poetic melting pot of many nations, the birthplace of Levi's and McDonald's. Lucky for you, there are over a thousand colleges to choose from, and American colleges have a special penchant for foreign exchange, constantly trying to send their own students to far-off lands for a semester or two of cultural education. We have a long history of welcoming outsiders here. So come on over—you'll be greeted with open arms.

Into the Woods (a.k.a., the Admissions Office)

As an overseas applicant, you have an inherent advantage in the admissions offices of America. American Universities want their campuses to be diverse places where people learn from each other as much as from professors and classes. The more diverse a learning environment is, the more enriching it's considered, so colleges want to create the most diverse student populations they can. And you, whether you think so or not, are living, breathing, walking diversity. Each year universities put enormous time and effort into recruiting international students, which can only work in your favor. So congratulations! The U.S. wants *you*.

Study Abroad vs. Four Years Abroad

Before you start jumping for those applications, it's important to consider your reasons for pursuing an education abroad. Just because you want to go to school in America doesn't mean that you have to do all four years here. (America's a cool place and all, but other places are cool, too.)

Many American universities participate in study abroad programs, both hosting and sending students to and from foreign universities for a semester or two at a time. Study abroad programs offer temporary immersion in American culture on a more short-term basis, with a wide variety of programs to choose from. Some programs will have you in classes alongside American students, while others will have their students in their own language-intensive classes. Many programs include specialty academic curricula, as well as fun sightseeing trips to various points of interest, such as the Statue of Liberty, the Smithsonian, and Hooters bars. All right, that last one is extracurricular, but in any case, you'll have lots of options to choose from.

Though most existing study abroad programs are agreements between an American university and a foreign university, if your home university doesn't participate in an American study abroad program, feel free to contact an American school for information. Many schools will happily make exceptions for individual students.

Is This Really for Me?

To help decide whether or not a longer stay abroad would be to your advantage, ask yourself some basic questions. Why are you interested in higher education in America? What do you hope to gain out of your time abroad? Does your home country contain educational opportunities that fit your needs, or can these needs be better met in the U.S.?

Whether you chose the study abroad or four years abroad option is completely up to your personal preferences, though you should be aware of both options.

A number of universities host summer study abroad programs, allowing you to visit America and gain academic credit for just

While in 1975 there were only 180,000 international students in American colleges, by 1997 that figure rose to 460,000.

Source: www.idahoea.org

three months. These programs can often help students decide whether or not they really want to pursue a longer study abroad program. Many summer programs accept high school students, an option we highly recommend before applying to American colleges, if feasible. Not only will a summer high school experience abroad allow you to see if you really like the States or not, but the colleges to which you apply will see that you're serious and independent, and have adjusted to American life in the past. You'll also return for your college education with a much better idea of what to expect, decreasing any adjustment issues you may have later on.

Differences Between International and U.S. Universities

Before you start applying, there are some fundamental differences between American universities and international universities that deserve comment. For starters, most American universities are not government regulated or funded. This means that the quality of education varies largely from university to university—some colleges are known for their intellectual vigor and others for their mass beer consumption. Knowing this, it's pivotal to make sure that the schools you're applying to have the same focus that you do, because if you're intellectually vigorous, you're going to be miserable in Beer Land.

Unlike in many schools in other countries, academics is not always the sole focus of an undergraduate education in America,

FREELY FOOTING THE BILL   **241**

and schools will recruit students accordingly. Colleges differ in their overall educational vision, i.e. what the administration's goals are. For example, some schools, such as Julliard, are known for their music programs, and focus on recruiting fabulous instrumental soloists and composers. Other schools are known for their athletic programs, and will recruit phenomenal athletes whose academic skills might be lacking. Some schools focus almost entirely on academics, as though their mantra were, "send us your nerds." All American universities are not equal, not even close, and international students should pay particular care to the kind of school to which they're applying, because there's nothing worse than being a Bookworm in Beach Country.

Equally important is the campus atmosphere. Each university has its own ambiance, resulting in the types of students who choose to go there. You can be sure that the day-to-day atmosphere at Julliard differs vastly from the general nerd-feel of the California Institute of Technology and the beach-party feel of the University of Southern California. This said, visit! Many foreign students underestimate the importance of visiting schools before accepting those thick envelopes, because schools in their home country are all similar. If you can, visit!

Freely Footing the Bill

Because most American colleges are not government funded, American high school graduates are free to choose their own universities—and pay for them. Unlike most other countries, the U.S.

Looking for other non-locals? During the fall 2001 semester, 4,695 international students from 132 countries studied at the West Lafayette campus of Purdue University, the highest percentage in the country that year.

has no nationalized higher education system. (America is big on individual rights, and seems to have large issues with nationalizing anything, whether it be education or healthcare or childcare.) With no nationalized anything, life is something of a free-for-all for everyone involved. You can pretty much expect to be in control of most aspects of your life, with the exception of your sky-rocketing tuition bills. Here's the lowdown:

State and Private

The annual tuition for different schools varies drastically. State schools tend to have cheap tuitions for in-state residents, and comparatively obscene rates for out-of-staters. Largely funded by in-state taxpayers and federal funding, state schools usually recruit from their home states, guaranteeing acceptance to academically strong students. With such a big difference between in-state and out-of-state tuitions, there are always large debates surrounding the laws that consider a student "in-state." Although rest assured, as a foreigner, you're never going to be considered in-state. The only loophole is if your family purchases land and receives mail at a residence in the state you choose four years before you're ready to go to college in that state. If you're wealthy enough and *that* committed to going to school in Arizona, by all means, buy up that land! But really, it won't save you that much in the long run, so we recommend just paying the out-of-state tuition and being proud that you're from far away. After all, not everyone can be from Arizona, and the people in Arizona would probably love to meet people from way out of town.

If you want to attend an American college but still spend some time in your homeland, think about attending St. Olaf College in Northfield, Minnesota, which in the 1998–1999 school year sent 632 students abroad, the same number as a typical graduating class!

Students from Russia who want to go to college in America have to prove to the American consulate that they have a reason to return to Russia when they graduate.

Source: The Daily Free Press.

It is worth mentioning that not all state schools are created equal. There is a large range in quality of education within state school systems, so the State University of New York (SUNY) at Binghamton may well be far superior to SUNY Plattsburg, even though they have the same name.

Private schools—this is intuitive—are schools financed by private funds. Private schools generally sustain themselves through high tuition rates and lots of fundraising among rich alumni, though, as you'll soon find out, they also like to badger not-so-rich alumni, like yourself eight weeks after graduation. Most universities do actually pick up small amounts of state and government funding, such as work-study programs, but these funds are minimal in comparison to the endowment required to run a university.

In most cases, private schools can afford more money per student, which translates into more individualized attention. Private schools invariably make up the top bundle of schools in the annual rankings, with the exception of the University of California at Berkeley and the University of Virginia, both of which are known for their public school excellence. Private schools will also have more student diversity, drawing more students from a wider demographic range, which may create a more comfortable environment for international students.

Financial Aid, Please

Financial aid to overseas students depends on the college. The major public universities don't usually offer aid to international students whatsoever. Some schools, such as Harvard, Middlebury, and Princeton, don't differentiate between national and international aid—these schools are considered "need blind" and will help you out financially if they decide to accept you. Other schools, such as Cal Tech, regularly offer financial aid to foreign students, but are "need-sensitive," i.e., they keep your financial status in mind throughout the admissions process, and might lean toward more well-off students.

Most schools cap their aid to international students, meaning that there's a finite limit to how much aid international students are offered each year. As a general rule, find out your college's financial aid policy toward international students as early as possible. (The early bird catches the fattest scholarship.)

Since very few international students will get free scholar-ships, your family's ability to pay your tuition bills is fully depen-dent on the international currency exchange rates. Many schools will require some form of proof that you can pay. But just because you can pay now doesn't mean you'll be able to pay next year. If your country's economy tanks, for instance, your currency might be worth pennies when converted into American dollars. Or vice versa, your currency might become very strong, allowing you to buy lots of cool CDs. So plan ahead and expect changes in the world market to come up. It might be a good idea to transfer funds to the U.S. while you're in school, since the fluctuations within our economy will affect the price of your tuition in a pre-dictable way. Your admissions office should have ideas for how to ensure your family's continued ability to foot your bills, such as keeping money in foreign banks, so ask.

Also, make sure to fill out those financial aid forms for schools that offer aid to international students, regardless of how well-off your family might be in your home country. If the exchange rate is lacking in your direction, you'll seem poor in the eyes of an American financial aid office and can pick up a fat financial scholarship. If your family will be financially strained under your college bills, look for funding in your own country. Government programs, private foundations, companies, or alumni may offer educational funding not restricted to your home country, or specifically geared toward education abroad. Milk 'em for all they're worth.

Checklist for Choosing a School

Important information and ideas to consider about prospective American schools:

Check the percentages of foreign students at your prospective university. These figures are usually available on college websites. Be sure to check out the specific breakdown of those international students. For example, if a school is 25 percent international students, but 24 percent of students are of Canadian origin, the university might not be as international as you thought at first glance. Decide what you want in a school whether it be more familiar-looking faces or more immersion in American culture. If the numbers that you find don't give you a clear enough picture, don't be hesitant to call up and ask someone. After all, an American college is a big leap and you ought to at least know the kind of water you're jumping into.

Create a student contact through your prospective school's international office, preferably a student from your home country. This is the best way to get a firsthand account of what a prospective university is like for someone of your native culture. International students are usually happy to recruit their own countrymen and women, and will be very helpful.

Keep in mind that schools of international renown will be harder to get into than other schools. Many international students have only heard of one or two premier American universities, and are unaware of the other thousand institutions of higher learning. This means that entrance into Boston College will be

On October 17, 2000, President Clinton signed a law removing the cap on the number of international employees universities are allowed to have— this includes teaching assistants and lab workers.

easier than entrance into California Institute of Technology, which will be easier than entrance into Harvard University. Highly selective schools tend to have stricter international quotas, meaning that only a certain percentage of their student body can be international students. With this in mind, make sure you plan to apply to a "safety school" that will most likely accept you.

Be aware of current feelings on your prospective campus toward international students. For example, the increasing number of foreign athletes going to school on American scholarships over the past decade has been an issue of hot contention, so if you're an athlete, you might want to ask a current student how you would be received.

Keeping abreast of your country's foreign affairs situation is also a good idea, just to be aware of any prejudices you may encounter. For example, many Middle Eastern students may encounter unwarranted prejudice at certain American Universities because of U.S. military involvement there, both at present and in the last decade. It is an unfortunate thing to have to consider, and we hope that you face no prejudice while at U.S. colleges, but you might, and you should be aware of it before you come. If possible, talk to students on-campus about what the atmosphere is like for students of Middle Eastern descent. If a college is particularly hostile, it's up to you to either avoid the place for your comfort and safety, or go right in there and teach those guys a thing or two about what a fun-loving, peace-celebrating person you can be. Boo-ya.

The Eight Golden Rules of International Applications

(1) Start ridiculously early, 24 months early if possible. Get copies of applications years in advance, just to make sure you know what's expected of you. This is the only way to ensure that both you and your college receive all the necessary information in a timely manner. Both the international mail system and college admissions offices are known for losing documents pivotal to your future, and given the extra distance, it will take both ends much longer to inform each other when they don't have what they need.

(2) With this in mind, it is *crucial* that you keep extra copies of all parts of your application, so that when your school contacts you

saying what they don't have (and they will), you can easily send another copy.

(3) Send all application materials weeks—if not months—early.

(4) If receiving or sending mail are a problem from your location, either fax your material or contact an admissions officer via email, and make an arrangement that way. School will probably send you an acceptance telegram, but do call to make sure they've received your app (expensive but worth it).

(5) Create an email contact in the admissions office with an international students officer. (Snail mail will only cause you grief, which is what we're trying to avoid.) This is the best way to prevent miscommunications and lost documentation. After you send in paperwork, double check to make sure it was received.

(6) Make sure to mention early on whether or not you're a United States citizen. Usually it's not hard—just answer the, "Are you a United States citizen?" question on their forms honestly. This is pivotal legal information for the admissions office.

(7) If you can't get money out of your country to pay application fees, your college might waive its application fee altogether. Just send an explanatory note along with your application and if there's a problem, you'll be contacted.

(8) If your academic transcript is not in English, send your school an official translation. These translations usually need to be officially certified, so ask your contact in the international students office what your school's specifications are.

In summary, the early bird with good organizational skills catches the acceptance package.

Spinning Yourself

As an international student, you have a slight competitive edge because you're *wanted*—all American universities seek diversity. It's nice to be wanted. However, you need to make sure to use that diversity to your advantage in your application.

While run-of-the-mill American high school students struggle to create unique application identities that will make them stand out in admissions, you're already unique just because of where you live. This is a huge bonus. However, once your application lands in an admissions office, you'll be compared to the other applicants from your region who might be equally diverse, and not to boring Americans. This means that you need to take advantage of the situation by proving that you'll be able to fit in at an American school. By emphasizing your differences, while assuring that you'll be comfortable in an American university, you'll placate the admissions office's fear that you'll not adjust well.

For example, you might want to show how your unique background will serve you in your new and unique environment. This strategy will make you shine in comparison to your region's applicants as a mature combination of diversity and assimilation. Feel free to be funny, but make sure the humor translates.

You can also take advantage of any application question asking where you've lived previously. If you have lived in the U.S. for a short time, even a few weeks, say so. Turn this minor question into an opportunity to mention how much you loved it, and how much you want to come back.

Also, rest assured that you will be judged alongside the values and opportunities offered in your region. So, if participating in extracurricular activities in your country is not the norm, your lack of participation will not be held against you in the way it would be against an American applicant. By the same token, if the offerings of your immediate locale differ from that of your country at large, you may want to address the issue directly with your contact in the admissions office, just to ensure that they're aware of your opportunities, or lack thereof.

A Note to Canadians

Many colleges continue to classify you Canucks as "international students," even though you're about as foreign as Coca-Cola. We're on to you. And we don't know why college admissions offices aren't, though we're assuming that by considering you foreigners, universities are able to boost their diversity statistics. So take advantage of it, and play the "I'll fit in well in America" card for all it's worth.

Testing Requirements

Most universities require TOEFL (Test of English as a Foreign Language) scores for international students. The exam tests your grasp of the English language, so if you're not fluent, you may well bomb it. Some schools will accept low TOEFL scores with the understanding that you're going to take an intensive English course upon arrival, but such agreements need to be made far ahead of time. The decision of whether to take an intensive English course at home or in America is an important one. It will probably be cheaper in your home country, but provide a better introduction if taken in America, especially with complete immersion in the language. It's up to you.

Many schools also require the TWE (Test of Written English), which is a sub-test of the TOEFL, but is not always offered with every administering of the TOEFL. We don't really understand why this is so unnecessarily complicated, but as always, we recommend that you make sure you're registered for the tests required by your schools. The

Is music the universal language? You'd think so, because 40 percent of the students at Berklee College of Music in Boston are international students.

International students send seven billion dollars into the economy each year.

ELPT (SAT II English Language Proficiency Test) can sometimes be taken instead of the TOEFL, as can the MELAB (Michigan English Language Assessment Battery), though the TOEFL is usually preferred. (For more on the TOEFL, see page 43.)

An ACT or SAT I test is also required for admission to most colleges. If it's impossible for you to take such a test in your country, contact the admissions office as soon as possible to see if they can recommend a supplementary exam. Otherwise, pick up a study guide and study away. If English isn't your first language, don't worry—colleges will understand low scores, particularly on the verbal section. Secondary education in other countries isn't geared toward the SAT I and ACT like American high school educations are, and this is understood by everyone involved, so do your best and don't sweat it! (For more on the SAT and ACT, see page 32.)

As for any other upper-school testing you may take in your home country, make sure to send in your results because they may place you out of college classes. American students will often use Advanced Placement and International Baccalaureate scores to get credit for college material they've already learned. Don't sell yourself short—though most universities won't accept foreign testing, it's always worth a try. Once you arrive on campus, if you feel that taking a course would be a waste of time and you've already been tested on the material, take a trip down to a dean's office to discuss your options. An in-person meeting to tell a sob story always helps, because believe it or not, administrators have consciences, too.

Post-Acceptance Paperwork

Once you're in, if you want to see any parts of America besides the airport immigration holding area, you need to obtain a student visa. You'll need an I-20 Form, which is the certificate of eligibility that's used to apply for a student visa at your home U.S. embassy. If you need a passport, your college will give you details.

Like all paperwork that involves multiple countries, these forms have the potential to be a documentation disaster, so proceed with speed, caution, and extra copies of everything (especially the passport part). Our advice: Start early and pray regularly.

As of the 1999–2000 school year, 43 percent of foreign scholars in the United States hailed from Asia.

Source: The Institute of International Education

Key Points Before You Go

Make sure you have a room assignment and a meal plan. We can't emphasize these points enough. Start double checking as soon as you're accepted, because there's nothing worse than arriving in a foreign country and finding out that you have no place to sleep and nothing to eat.

Make sure you have health insurance. You'll want to find out your healthcare options long before you catch your school's Freshman Plague, which usually comes in the form of a debilitating autumn stomach bug. Though we joke, this is serious stuff.

Find out what your employment options are. Don't assume that you're eligible for employment in America and will be easily able to supplement your family's income. Employment rules are annoyingly strict and confusing over who can work in the States—you may be ineligible if you're not a U.S. citizen, depending on the terms of your visa. Ask your international students office.

Culture Shock

International students are expected to have some surprises in the process of adjusting to their new environments. For this reason, most schools have some sort of International Student club, through which you can make friends, gain a strong source of support, and obtain occasional free chocolate chip cookies. International student clubs often create a family of students with whom you'll bond and hang out, making the transition to daily American chaos much easier to handle. Obviously, if you're a Canuck who grew up two miles north of New York State, your adjustment will be minor compared to that of a student from a country whose average monthly income is $40. Still, we can give you a head's up on some of those unexpected, strange American habits:

Those Loose Learners

International students are often surprised at the lax relationships that exist between students and professors in the United States. Many universities strive to make professors easily accessible to students, so it's not unusual to see relaxed classroom environments, or haphazardly dressed students eating lunch with their teachers in university cafeterias, speaking colloquially. Such scenes would be unheard of in France, for instance, where students dress well for class, professors are addressed with the most formal of language, and everyone eats baguettes. (And sometimes frogs, but that's another story.) American education has its own culture, and you should expect to adjust accordingly.

All-American Attitude

Americans place a strong emphasis on choosing a school that's "right for you," as opposed to the best school you can get into. In the words of one international student, "Where I come from, happiness isn't really a consideration." In America, it's the main consideration. Students will visit ten schools just to make sure that their number one school "feels right."

In addition to the general emphasis on happiness, many international students are surprised to find more broad-based cultural differences. American schools, for example, tend to value well-rounded students much more than strictly academic students. This means that many students will spend their free time juggling commitments to academics, a sport, an extracurricular club, and a part-time job. While this kind of balancing act is status quo in America, if you come from a country where high schoolers just don't do sports or work part-time, the schedules of your fellow students will look ridiculous. (Never fear, soon your schedule will be just like theirs.)

Student Life

American day-to-day customs may differ from what you're used to. Drinking alcoholic beverages is illegal until age 21 here, which may well be (or at least feel like) the strictest drinking age in the world. (Don't worry, many people ignore that rule.) College kids usually stay up 'til all hours of the night, with minimal sleep and maximum co-ed mingling, studying, and partying. Sexuality tends to be somewhat free, with free condom bins popular on many campuses and random "hook-ups" a college-life norm. Expect these differences, and feel free to join the fun.

Clothes

Unless you've already visited your college, we recommend that you hold off on purchasing clothes until you arrive on campus so you can see the popular styles. Don't assume that students dress well for class—one Harvard University security guard once commented that he can't always tell who's a student and who's trespassing because the students dress like they're homeless. This said, it's better to wait and see. Also, the weather on your new campus may be very different from what you're used to, so purchase appropriately. (No matter how cute that red tank top is, you're going to be hating life during January's blizzards.)

Vacations

Keep in mind that most American universities' dorms close during vacations, meaning you'll have to find somewhere else to go. Each school's schedule is different, but most have a host-family program through the international student office that allows you to spend the holidays with a nearby family if it's too expensive or complicated for you to go home. (For example, it takes 28 hours to fly home and Thanksgiving vacation is only four days long, so you're probably not going home.) Many American students stick around for vacations, too, either to avoid their families or the hassle and expense of traveling. It's not at all a big deal, so enjoy the chance to relax and catch up on homework, sleep, and movies.

CHAPTER ELEVEN

Getting the News

The Envelope Approacheth

So you've chased down the mail woman for the umpteenth time, but today she has the envelope. All of your dreams are pressed here between some paper and foul-tasting glue, marked with a return address from the school of your dreams. Bulk-rate-beautiful. But wait, this envelope seems a little bit thin. Have you been rejected, or are Harvard admissions' envelopes unusually thin in order to mess with your mind one last time? (They are, in fact.) Just take a breath and look at your answer, then read on to deal with the consequences.

"Thank You For Playing— Please Try Again"

Strategies for Dealing with Rejection

So things didn't quite work out this time. First of all, try to take it with grace. If anyone asks you if you got in, make up some lie about how you didn't even look to see because you realized that school's so dumb and full of jerks and you wish you never even heard of them. Then burn the rejection letter in a ritualistic manner that curses the admissions officers to an eternal habitation of fleas in their underwear drawer. Heh, heh, heh . . .

Collect yourself. You applied to several schools, right? There's nothing wrong with not going to your top choice. Remember that story about the guy who went to Princeton and ended up going crazy? No? Well that really happened, and that could have been you!

This might be your first time facing serious rejection, in which case you might wonder if you're really as smart as you thought you were. Don't worry, you are! Just because you didn't get into every school you applied to doesn't mean that you're an idiot. After all, once the acceptance letters from other colleges start coming in, you'll realize that you're still smarter than the people who didn't get into the schools where you *were* accepted!

In all seriousness, don't equate college acceptance with any sort of abstract conception of worth. Admissions officials will tell you that there is certainly an element of luck in the process. (For example, the part where they spin a big roulette wheel and admit every applicant whose SAT Verbal score matches the number it lands on.) Some people just happen to catch the eye of the handful of stodgy, senile academics who go through your applications, and some don't. There might be any number of arbitrary circumstances that went into the decision, which you will never understand and could not possibly have prevented. Admissions is not a perfect science by any stretch, and the people making the decisions are flawed because they're human. Your application might have caused heated debate in the last-round committee meeting, and your admissions officer might have shed tears while arguing in your favor only to be overturned in the eleventh hour by the director who was suffering (unbeknownst to him) from a ruptured appendix and later rushed to the hospital. Alas, you'll never know, so there's no sense in obsessing over the hows and whys.

Finally, remember not to take the school's decision personally. They don't know you. They don't know how you never fail to remember your friends' birthdays. They don't even know how cool you are at parties, unless that's what you wrote your essay about. All they have in front of them to judge you by are a series of numbers and some words on paper that may or may not portray you well. They didn't reject you,

Although you might think you won't get in anywhere, don't get discouraged. In 2000, 14.9 million students were enrolled in U.S. universities.

Source: www.idahoea.org

While in 1982, 9 percent of student aid was not need-based, today it is 16.8 percent.

Source: Focusing on Higher Education Today

they rejected applicant #15,306 because that day they didn't want to read any more essays about sports, or because one of the initial reviewers thinks that everyone admitted to their school ought to have taken five or more APs.

So do your best to get over it. They suck anyway. Look on the bright side, and focus on the schools you did get into. Now, *they* all want *you*, not the other way around.

An Extremely Short Glossary of Terms for Rejection

DEFERRED. If you get deferred, it means that the school isn't sure about whether it plans to accept you if you applied early, so you'll have to wait until the spring and hear along with everyone else. Your initial reaction to learning you're deferred will most likely be one of disappointment, but don't fret. Some deferred people definitely *do* end up getting accepted, and at least you didn't get outright rejected like some poor souls. Take a deferral for what it is, nothing more and nothing less. Don't get your hopes up, and don't let the admissions people mess with your head. If your early application was a binding one ("Early Decision," as opposed to "Early Action"), getting deferred does not bind you to the school's decision in the spring. Do your best in your fall classes and try to lead your soccer division in saves to increase your chances of getting bumped up to the Promised Land. Most important, apply to more schools. Cal Tech, specifically. You are so good at math!

WAITLISTED. If you get waitlisted, it means the school wants you (and your tuition money), but there are also other people they want, and when it came down to it, they just couldn't take as many applicants as they wanted, and you're the odd man out. However, if they find that some of the people they accepted decided to go to Cal Tech instead, one of their spots just might go to you! If you are waitlisted by one of your top choices, reply to their letter and let them know that you'd like to stay in contention, and they'll let you know, hopefully before you have to reply to the other schools that did accept you. Like your friends who were deferred, you're justified in clinging to the shred of hope that you'll make it aboard, but be prepared to go to another one of your choices in case things don't work out.

Calls from the Governor—Getting Off the Waitlist

Even though waitlists are ranked, many colleges will let you do things to improve your chances of getting off the waitlist (in the good acceptance way, not the bad rejection way). Call up the admissions office of the school that waitlisted you and ask if they accept additional materials (recommendations, new achievements, new transcripts) during the waiting period.

If so, send them your latest transcript if it would update their records for the better. Show them the higher score you got when you took the SAT drunk just for fun after you handed in all your applications. Let them know of any big recent accomplishment

The American Association of Community Colleges lists over 20 current members of Congress who got their higher education start in Community College.

you had in the winter or spring, such as how you led your Quizbowl team to the Nationals, developed a vaccine for a rare tropical disease, or single-handedly solved the world's overpopulation problem. Try to get someone to write an additional recommendation for you, perhaps the woman whose quadruplets you saved from that burning building. If you are lucky enough to be tight with an alum or faculty member of the school, try getting him or her to write you a recommendation. Although in all fairness it shouldn't, highlighting for them that you are the son of the Dean of the Engineering School just might stack the odds in your favor.

The Z-List

Some schools have what is referred to as a Z-list. This list of applicants has been admitted to the school, but not for the following fall. The college here has decided, for whatever reason, that these applicants would stand to benefit from a year off before attending. Z-list placements are often sent out to people who graduate from high school exceedingly early with respect to their age, or to people who have had very recent trauma in their life and who might need more time to deal with that before leaving home. Of course, sometimes there's no apparent reason. If you get Z-listed at your top-choice school, we recommend being happy—this is your opportunity to beg your parents for cash to go globe hopping, or to just hang around the house for a year while still telling everyone that you got in.

"Do You Want Fries With That?"— Coping with the Worst of Rejections

So you didn't get into your top school. Or any of the other schools you applied to. OK, you got into that one school, but your ex-boyfriend's going there and you might end up in a class with him if you went there, which would be really awkward, plus he'd think you were following him because you want him back. The bottom line is that things didn't work out as you planned, and you face the prospect of not going to college next year.

Awesome! No more school! Think of the things you could do with all your free time! You could go to fast food restaurants and sneer at the "Folklore and Mythology" majors who find themselves constantly arguing with their parents about the uselessness of their college degrees. At basketball games you could root against North Carolina *and* Duke, because they *both* rejected your

In one recent year, Harvard accepted only 11 percent of its applicant pool, of which 50 percent had SAT scores over 1400 and 16 percent were ranked at the top of their class.

Source: U.S. News and World Report

Want to go to U. Penn? Better apply before it is mathematically impossible to get in. In one recent year, their acceptance rate dropped from 31 percent to 22 percent.

Source: Focusing on Higher Education Today

application. You could travel the world, see movies, move into your own place, find yourself unable to travel the world because you don't have any money, get a job as a flight attendant for an international airline, encourage the union to strike, causing Cornell University admissions office employees to miss their flights, and read all the books you ever wanted. In short, you could live the good life.

But Seriously, Your Other Options

This is not the end of your education, and if you really want that degree, don't let this round of rejections stop you. Have you considered community college? While there, you could improve your student reputation and maybe get into one of your choice schools before graduation—no employer would ever know the difference. You could also take some time off to do interesting, meaningful things—like join the peace corps or work on your novel—after a year, you could try again and this time, you'd have another year of life and maturity on your side!

For the Fat Envelopes: Choosing from Many Options

Maybe you got accepted to not only your top-choice college, but to more than one of your dream schools and now you have to choose. Poor you.

The best advice we can give you is to start the process by comparing the packages each school offers. Keep travel expenses and phone bills in mind. Now you and your parents can have a nice healthy debate about where you belong. If you got a free ride somewhere, they'll want good reasons why you don't want to go there, and you should hear them out. Life without debt is the good life. In the end, you should really know where you want to go by heart. Is there one school that, if you turn it down, you will ask yourself every day for the rest of your life why you didn't go there? Maybe it would be easier to not have to ask. One student, who had accepted a prestigious full scholarship at a top university commented, "About once a week I used to think about what was going on at Harvard right then. It isn't that I didn't love my college, it's just that I think I would have loved Harvard more." Before you let money make the decision for you, see our finance section for more information on playing the money game.

While the most competitive schools in the country accept around 10 percent of applicants, the Julliard School of New York is still slightly more selective, turning away a full 92 percent of applicants each year.

The Reply Card

So much excitement and promise in such a tiny card, the reply card needs only a check, a signature, and a stamp to guarantee your place at the school of your dreams. No need to be fancy—they just want to know if you're coming. There are, however, a few things you should know about those little cards.

Send in cards from schools that you don't want to attend as soon as possible. The school is waiting to hear from you before it lets in other kids off the waitlist, and it's just cruel of you to take up a spot on their admit list longer than need be, while some poor kid gets ever closer to insanity waiting to hear.

Don't you dare respond "yes" to more than one school. Many colleges communicate with each other after admissions time and if you come up on more than one list of incoming students, you'll be in a lot of trouble—enough that one or both colleges might rescind their offer of admission.

If you lose that card, they really don't care that much. It's just for bookkeeping purposes, anyway, so feel free to just call the admissions office of the school you're going to attend and tell them.

Send in the card ON TIME! Even if your decision takes agonizing nights to complete, you are obligated to send in that card! With no notice of your position by the reply date, the admissions office WILL ASSUME that you don't want to go there. Don't let this happen—you've come so far already!

Taking Time Off

At many schools, reply cards feature the check-box option of taking a year off before entering college. This is another great way

If you don't get into your top choice, one thing you can blame is grade inflation— the GPAs of every other applicant are probably just inflated. In a recent study, 34 percent of college students said they had an "A" average in high school and 12 percent said they had a "C" average, compared to 12.5 percent and 32.5 percent in 1960.

Source: Focusing on Higher Education Today

Mad because you have to wait around for three years at college before you can drink? Imagine how Gregory Smith of Randolph Macon College in Virginia feels: he started his freshman year in 1999 at age 10!

---

to help out those kids on the waitlist if you want to take some time off. You really ought to consider it before laughing it off as something for the idle or the rich. One junior here at Harvard notes, "taking a year off was the best thing I ever did—I had time to do cool things before starting the whole school thing, and I turned 21 before anyone else in my class!" A year of time before college has the advantage of letting you mature a bit more before entering a new environment, but you should also keep in mind the downside. It will be five years now before you'll be out of your undergraduate career. If this seems scary and far away, maybe you should just head off to college. On the other hand, it might be appealing to stay out of the real world for as long as possible, in which case, this is another way to stall participation in the work-a-day world to come.

CHAPTER TWELVE

The Post-Acceptance Party

Some Good Advice Before You Go

So you have gained acceptance into the college of your dreams. Congratulations! Start the party! Go crazy! Get it on! Go nuts!

Wait, wait, no, that's a bad idea. An awful idea. Horrible idea. (As Harvard students, we should know better.)

The whole "party" idea needs to be held off for another few months because your college accepted you with the understanding that your senior spring behavior would closely mimic your previous conduct. Unfortunately, your high school is required to report your second semester grades to colleges, as well as any behavioral discretion. Colleges have been known to retract acceptance offerings from those who can't be trusted to behave appropriately, instead giving their last dwindling spots to anxious waitlisters.

Risky Behavior/Things to Avoid During Senior Spring
Anything that ends with the sound "shun": Detention, suspension, conviction, etc.
All substances that are either illegal or require proof that you're approximately three years older than you are to consume it.
Any grade starting with the letters "C" or "D."
Anything that involves cops (contrary to the teachings of DARE, the men in blue are not your friends).

Deviances that involve questions of integrity, such as academic dishonesty, will be given especially harsh consideration by colleges. This is particularly true at schools with an honor code, where students frequently take important exams without proctors. (Summary: Don't cheat.)

If you are misguided enough to mistakenly demonstrate some form of poor behavior that will be reported to your college, write a letter to your college *before they request one* (they're going to request one), explaining as candidly as possible what happened, how remorseful you are, and why you still deserve to be a member of their incoming freshman class. Portray yourself in the most positive light possible, while being nothing short of hyper-formal, hyper-truthful and hyper-guilt-ridden. Your honesty will be looked upon favorably by the admissions committee and may well save your misbehaving butt.

The same is recommended for poor grades, particularly Ds. If you have a C or D in one class, a letter is not really necessary, though check with your college counselor. However, if you display an overall plummeting of grades due to having prematurely begun the Post-Acceptance Party, you need to come up with a *great personal excuse* explaining your downhill slide, then write a letter employing this excuse.

It is much easier to keep your grades and behavior in check in the first place than it is to explain to an admissions committee why you're having so much fun, even if you are just overjoyed at the prospect of attending college and simply want to vent this joy in party-like fashion. Leave the partying 'til June.

The Housing Form Crapshoot

Sometime between May and July, housing forms should arrive from your university. We highly recommend that freshmen take

great personal excuse

1. A seemingly honest explanation for your recent academic difficulties.

2. A dispelling of the myth that your grade dive correlates with your acceptance to college.

3. An elaboration of sudden personal problems, existent or non-existent.

4. "I've been partying a lot lately" is not a great personal excuse.

on-campus housing if it's offered. You'll be living in off-campus housing for the rest of your life, and freshmen rooming tends to be a bonding experience as well as an automatic means of participating in campus life. It's important to create that first link to your campus, and housing forces it. It's also kind of fun. Whatever your do, make sure to mail in your housing form by its due date, or else your pairing will take place with no information, a potentially disastrous situation.

Forms vary by university. Some just want to know if you're a smoker, others if you'd mind living with a smoker, and still more, the deep secrets of your personal life. How these forms are actually used once you mail them back varies as much as the forms themselves, usually depending on the individual deans in charge of rooming. For some deans, creating rooming lists is an art. For others, rooming is a great social experiment. For a special few, the process is as random as a drunken game of pin-the-tail-on-the-donkey.

All this variation should not inhibit you from ending up with an ideal roommate (read: a non-psycho). Experience shows that you really just want someone you can live with, not necessarily a best friend. The sanity level of your roommate will make or break your freshman year. Horror stories abound about Tan Tina, who insists on sleeping 14 hours a night with a 1000-watt sunlamp and cucumber slices over her eyes between full-volume, five-hour soap opera marathons. Or Hypersexual Howard, the roommate who brings home a different, noisy significant other every night, exiling you from your room (thus coining the term "sexile").

Trust us, you don't want Tan Tina or Hypersexual Howard. You want a roommate who's pleasant, tolerant, tolerable, reasonable, and easy to live with, so ask older students on your prefrosh visits, "Quite frankly, what do I need to do to not be roomed with a psycho?" They'll know. Example: "I think I put something about wanting to talk about politics," says a friendly Harvard student dispelling advice. "Don't do that."

The best strategy for filling out your forms is to avoid all *extreme* answers, regardless of the question.

You may think you're an extreme, but really, you're not. You might think that you're loud, but clearly you haven't met Tanker Tom, your new klutzy 400 pound roommate with a hearing problem and a passion for heavy metal; the type that evacuates the building when he falls because students think a bomb went off.

extreme

1. Portraying your traits as excessive.

2. "I am a morning person."

3. "I am very social."

4. "I am a slob."

5. "I am very loud."

6. "I am a heavy smoker."

Think moderation. There are a surprising number of college students who were normal before college, but when left to their own devices, are very extreme (read: crazy). Many smooth out after a couple years of college, but this doesn't help you for your first year. And if you're not careful, you will be roomed with these people.

Things You Didn't Know About Yourself: Form-Filler Tips

Sleep

Your college sleep schedule will probably be reminiscent of your current weekend schedule. It will most likely bear little to no resemblance to your current high school–induced schedule, we promise. If you wake up before noon on Saturdays, you're a morning person ("A.M."). If you go to bed anytime after midnight, your bedtime will probably shift to the dawn-hours once you hit university life ("P.M."). If you have insomnia, star that, and beg for a person with quiet, rest-oriented habits. Take these guidelines to heart, because pairing the kid who awakes to loud music at 5 A.M. with an insomniac who needs silence for slumber and finally drifts off to sleep around 4 A.M. will be nothing short of disastrous for everyone involved.

Cleanliness

Go with the cleanliness level you'd like your roommate to be, keeping in mind that people claim to be neater than they really are. If you think you're a slob, we promise, you're not—if you've seen your bedroom floor in the past year, you're somewhere around average. Never go with the "super clean" option, because you'll end up paired with an obsessive-compulsive neat freak who gets upset if you rip a piece of paper because it sends millions of microscopic dust particles into the air. Moderation.

Social Levels

When in doubt, go with a happy medium. The extremes are more extreme than you could ever imagine. You may think you're bubbly and hyper-social, but if you value sleep, say you're moderately social. If you're quiet and sometimes withdrawn, you want to room with someone who will draw you out of your shell a bit, giving you a social life by default. In this case it's important to avoid the lowest social ranking because your social aspirations will probably improve in college. (Two quietly withdrawn roommates = two quietly miserable roommates.)

Oddities

If you're unusual, for the love of God, say so. Your oddities will probably draw an intolerant roommate into an immediate war pact against you, the last thing you need during freshman year. Also, idiosyncrasies only increase in college, and you want a roommate who's understanding (or even a practicer of) your unusual habits, so please be honest. The housing office doesn't want room wars, and will generally do everything possible to avoid them if you spell out your habits.

Sexuality

We have never heard of roommate problems caused by sexual orientation alone. Still, there are ways of hinting that you want a roommate who will be understanding of your lifestyle. (Universities tend to be particularly open to such suggestions because of the high potential for lawsuits in this arena.) Repeatedly requesting "tolerance" and "liberalism" should prevent you from being roomed with an all-out skinhead, and if you feel comfortable, it is all right to subtly come out on your housing form.

Keep in mind that there's a price for using the word "tolerant" any place on your housing form, as you may well end up with a roommate who requires massive amounts of tolerance.

Roommate Ruminations

Many schools allow you to request your number of future roommates. Rooming options themselves, in terms of floor plans, vary vastly from school to school, so make sure to check out some freshman dorms during your visits. There are pros and cons to ever rooming set-up, and this choice is purely up to your preferences, though your request may well be ignored by your university. (Harvard example: "I said that I'd like to room with athletes and wanted a lot of roommates, under the logic that I would bond with the athletes in the group. If the other roommates were crazy, we'd outnumber them and they'd be the ones to leave . . . Well, I got put in a double with a crazy instead.")

Quad or more

The more people you room with, the more likely you'll get along with someone. A large number of roommates also ensures always coming home to lots of people, a good way to prevent the home-sickness and loneliness that frequently plague freshmen. Keep in mind that your room will probably be a bit loud, just because of all the people bustling about at different hours. If you're shy or question your ability to bond with new friends, this option should be particularly attractive—after a few late-night study cri-ses, you may well have new lifelong friends. Additionally, the set-up of larger roommate groups (e.g. four rooms, six people) often allow students to get singles for at least part of the year, a major bonus. Conclusion: Go for it.

Triple

The success of a triple really depends largely on the floor plan—the more singles and fewer walk-through rooms, the better. Still, triples often end up pitting roommates against one another, with either of two possible outcomes: two roommates being the best of friends with one left out, or two roommates competing for the affections of Popular Pat, the roommate everyone adores. Con-clusion: Proceed with caution.

Double

It's a crapshoot. If you get along with your roommate, your life will be pleasant. If not, it could be borderline hellish. Doubles with two rooms are usually better off. Conclusion: It's a 50/50. If you don't want multiple roommates, go for it.

Single

There is nothing more depressing than going home to a completely empty room alone with ten hours to kill before bedtime. (They're dubbed "psycho singles" for a reason.) The single should be avoided particularly if you're not outgoing because you'll never make friends. We only recommend requesting a single if you're super outgoing and would prefer not to live on top of others, in which case you'll probably spend minimal time in your own room. Conclusion: Don't do it. If you do, at least check with current students beforehand.

Dorming Decisions

Many schools have special dorm options, such as single-sex dorms or dorms with mandatory quiet hours. If you're interested, think long and hard about the types of people who would request such dorms, and whether you would want to be their friends. Freshmen tend to make most of their friends on their halls, so the type of people who you choose to live around can have a heavy impact on your life.

Single-Sex Dorms

Better known as "vaults of virginity" or "lesbo land," most schools have limited student access to their all-female dorms as a safety precaution (i.e. your boy-friend can't come visit you, even if you want him to). However, many students simply feel more comfortable living with members of the same sex. The dynamic is vastly different from that of a co-ed dorm, but equally as fun. And, yes, it's socially acceptable to walk around in a towel. Conclu-sion: Before you check the "yes" box, check out the single-sex dorms on your visit.

Quiet Dorms

The rules surrounding quiet dorms vary from school to school—some are twenty-four-hour quiet dorms, while others are quiet only after 9 p.m. or 11 p.m. Regardless, you'll probably never host or attend a party in a quiet dorm, so, if this is a key part of your social plan, beware. If you're shy, a quiet dorm may not be the place for you. (It's very difficult to make friends when no

Don't think about this yet, but one-half of college gradu-ates have outstand-ing debts averaging $12,000.

Source: Focusing on Higher Education Today

---

medical exemption

1. A possibly but not necessarily legitimate way to ensure yourself ideal housing.

2. The methodology behind obtaining the ideal living situation, a single room within a suite.

---

one speaks.) If you're social but have trouble buckling down to schoolwork, a quiet dorm may help you concentrate. Bottom line: Only if you really need the quiet.

Chemical Free

These dorms ban all substances of bodily interest, namely drugs, alcohol, and cigarettes. Parties are more along the lines of "lets all watch a movie." Though you may be morally opposed to chemical use, you could always just say no in a regular dorm. Conclusion: A nice idea, but not really necessary.

The Medical Exemption

Colleges are required by law to provide, to the best of their ability, accommodating housing to disabled students. However, depending on the school, the term "disabled" varies greatly. For example, at many schools, the kid who's allergic to peanut products, or the kid with asthma whose condition is relatively mild, may well be able to request the very nice rooms nearby university health services, arguing proximity in case of an emergency. Check around to see where the nicest dorms are, and then find a reason why you need to live there—the insomniac from above might request a cushy room far from the always-loud highway, for example.

As long as a doctor writes you a note justifying your request, you're good to go. Though we don't recommend making up medical conditions (they'll catch you), do check your options with the university office of student disabilities.

The Rooming Info Is Assigned

So it's early August, your rooming assignment has arrived, and you're living in someplace called Butterwerg Hall (known to students as "The Butt"), with a roommate named Aruvia Yimsomaurivinti.

Don't worry if your dorm has a joke associated with it like "The Butt." Very often, the dorms with bad reputations aren't actually the ones to be feared. The truly awful dorms are so terrible that no one has the heart to make fun of 'em, so you won't know how bad it is 'til you live there. If you're desperate, you're welcome to call your dean in an effort to be put in better housing (they're required to be civil), but your efforts will probably be in vain, as housing deans are usually bombarded by ignorant prefrosh begging for

286 THE POST-ACCEPTANCE PARTY

conservative

1. Moderate.

2. Subdued.

3. Not weird.

4. Mindful that your strange habits, friends, and hobbies are still a secret.

5. Borderline dishonest.

6. You're super quirky.

room changes. If applicable, now would be a brilliant time to create a medical exemption (see "medical exemption").

As for your roommate, Aruvia Yimsomaurivinti, you should call or email. Calling is more direct and will give you a better idea of who you're rooming with, but email's safer—just make sure to limit the exclamation points. Example: "Hello! My name's Emily!!! I'm so excited that you're gonna be my roommate next year!!!! And we get to live in The Butt!!! I'm so excited to go to college!!! Aren't you???!!!" Emily is scary.

Whatever you do, be *conservative.*

First impressions are everything. Studies show that most people have made up their minds about you within the first five minutes of conversation. Do not scare your roommate. Aruvia already has enough to worry about.

Your main topic of discussion should be practical issues: who's bringing what? You should not assume that you'll get along with Aruvia well enough to share everything, but by the same token, you don't need multiple televisions, refrigerators, and irons. It's also considered a good-faith motion to offer to donate various items to the room. If your roommate lives near your college, he or she will be able to go home occasionally to get or drop off stuff. (If you get along, you may even get a home-cooked meal from time to time.) In the case of multiple roommates, email is ideal for the discussion of what to bring.

Course Confusion

Many schools still require course registration long before you ever set foot on campus. Best advice: Spend some time reading the coursebook and going over graduation requirements, making sure you're aware of what classes your AP exams have placed you out of. Select a tentative course plan, and then ask current students what they think. Talk to students who either share your academic background (such as alumni from your high school) or ones who share your interests and time constraints (such as members of a team or club you plan to join). They'll know all the gossip on individual courses. Whatever you decide, register *early*, as soon as possible.

Many courses are filled on a first-come, first serve basis, so if you want to be in a twenty-five-person class at a 30,000-person school, you'd better register early.

early

1. Before registration deadline.

2. Not after registration deadline.

3. As soon as you've chosen your courses, before registration deadline.

4. Not late.

Your freshman fall is not the time to worry about choosing a major, especially considering that the majority of college graduates do not graduate with degrees in their original field of interest. (Freshman chemistry, for example, often sends premeds flocking to the humanities by sophomore year.)

Instead, spend freshman fall taking the courses required for graduation, such as core curriculum courses or required freshmen writing classes. You can always choose interesting courses related to your major later on, but at this point, unless you personally know older students at your school, you don't have the information to make educated decisions about your courseload. (Many courses that look fabulous in the coursebook are actually quite hellish.) This way you'll save yourself from wasting precious electives. Also, many schools give incoming freshmen last priority in class selection, so you probably can't get into any fabulously interesting courses anyway.

The Ws of Course Selection

WHO: Who's teaching the course—a professor or a teaching assistant? You want professors, not teaching assistants, unless they come highly recommended. Do you have a rating guide for the teacher? Keep in mind that no matter how wonderful course material may sound, *don't* take a course where a teacher has a poor rating—you'll just hate life.

WHEN: Just say no to classes before 10am, because you won't be there unless you're honestly, without a doubt, a morning person It's best to write out a tentative course schedule, with ample free time for lunch, studying, and naps. (Eating and getting to class take much longer in college.) Also keep in mind that just because you attend high school every day now does not mean you're going to want to in college—think about schedule flexibility and days off. Don't schedule every free moment of your life, because you may well want to spontaneously watch a movie from time to time.

Also realize that labs can be incredibly time consuming, so that a class that meets two hours per week plus lab may well suck up over ten weekly hours of your precious time. Another hidden point: Many courses are only offered every other year, and you don't want to be waiting until your junior year to take a required class. Sometimes a course will say "to be taught by Professor X next year" or "not to be offered again" in small print at the bottom

If you want to catch a toga party before they all disappear, you'd better go to college quick! Membership in fraternities and sororities has decreased by 30 percent over the last decade.

Source: Focusing on Higher Education Today

of the description. Make sure you read all the small wording.

WHERE: Break out that campus map. Back-to-back courses on the other side of the world from each other will be annoying at best, and hellish when it's raining.

WHAT LEVEL: If you're not sure what level course you belong in, call the registrar's office and ask. You can place out of many introductory level courses with APs, but if your high school education was questionable, you may well want to take an introductory class to ensure that you know what's going on. Take recommended prerequisites seriously—they weren't typed into the course listing for the heck of it.

(W)HOW MANY: Do note how many students are in each class. It's recommended that freshmen take a variety of classes if possible, such as two large lecture classes, one medium-sized class, and one seminar course.

FRESHMEN SEMINARS: There's a growing trend in higher academia to offer special small seminars to freshmen, many of which are pass/fail. These seminars are often taught by faculty, and are among the most interesting courses offered. Even if they're by application only, apply—you'll thank yourself later.

SHOP THEN DROP: If you're allowed, try to apply for a couple extra courses, attend them for a few days, see which ones you like, and then drop the extras. *Do not* take more than the recommended courseload freshman fall. Though you may think you're academically amazing, you'll hate your courseload of four lab sciences and two "fun" English courses by November.

REMEMBER: Everything is flexible once you arrive on campus, no

create-a-conflict

1. A method of arranging your assigned class schedule to better meet your sleep requirements.

2. Example: "I'm sorry, but I babysit orphaned amoebas from 7 A.M. to 11 A.M. on Mondays and Wednesdays, and will not be able to attend your 8 A.M. class to which I have been assigned."

3. If #2 fails, create a medical exemption.

matter how inflexible administration claims to be. Professors will always be receptive to your "deep-rooted, lifelong interest" in their area of specialty, and will admit you to the class you were originally rejected from after a little prodding. (After all, the professor did devote his or her entire life to this one obscure subject.) If a class is full, go to the first meeting anyway, and then beg the professor for admittance. If a class has multiple sections and your teacher is not proficient in the English language, switch sections.

You can also always create a schedule conflict to avoid inconvenient scheduling. It's your education, so be pushy about it.

The Buying Bonanza

Chances are you've been mooching off your parents for approximately eighteen years now and will need to purchase some items of your own before going to college. Below is a list of the bare-minimum items to make sure you have. As for the items that are already rightfully yours, a good rule of thumb: if you haven't used or worn it in the past year, don't bring it. When in doubt over an obscure item, such as an ironing board, don't bring it (this is what floors are for). Your roommates will probably be naïve enough to bring lots of random belongings to school, such as turbo-powered irons, and before they decide to send them home after freshman year, you'll be able to use them.

Wardrobe

Clothing appropriate for *all* weather, including both warm and light jackets.

A few formal outfits.

Some crazy party clothes (what would you wear to a party with a country theme? A disco theme?).

Underwear. Lots and lots of underwear. That way you'll never have to do laundry.

A laundry bag or bin, detergent, and many rolls of quarters.

Socks. (see "underwear")

Umbrella and raingear.

Some form of jewelry, if applicable.

Weather-appropriate shoes.

Academics

A dictionary and thesaurus; foreign language dictionary.

A grammar guide (we like *The Elements of Style* and *The Write Source*).

Any books you used frequently for high school papers.

Many pencils, many pens, and many erasers, all of which will disappear by Christmas.

Scotch tape, duct tape, glue or gluestick.

Envelopes, stationary, stamps (of the current first-rate value—this is key).

Markers, crayons, and colored pencils to make you seem more creative than you are.

Rubber bands, paper clips, safety pins, mini-stapler, staples.

Academics

Extension cords and power strips, so you can plug in everything you own at once.

White-out.

General

A bowl and plate, some silverware (you'll eventually end up mooching from the dining hall).

Aspirin/Tylenol/Ibuprofen, cold medicine, cough drops (to help cure the inevitable Freshmen Plague).

Tissues, toothbrush, toothpaste, washcloth, towels, tweezers, soap, shampoo, conditioner, shower caddy.

Sheets, two sets. (The one-dirty, one-clean formula.) If you want your sheets to actually fit your bed, find out the size of college mattresses.

Lots of cosmetics and feminine supplies (unless you want to buy 'em at the ever-busy school store).

Alarm clock, watch.

Stereo, though many just use their computer to play music.

Refrigerator, microwave, coffee pot (optional, probably forbidden, but go for it if not).

Sleeping bag for guests.

Garbage pail.

Your wallet—money, real license/identification, fake license/identification, social security card.

Buying at Home vs. Buying at School

Though the stores around your school will most likely carry all the basic necessities, they tend to mark up the prices during the first month of school, especially for suckers like you. It may be cheaper to buy at school than ship though, especially items like refrigerators. If you are planning to buy at school, get there as early as possible, even a couple days early to stay in a hotel with your parents, so you'll have adequate time to shop before freshmen week. (You probably won't even have time to sleep during fresh-men week, much less shop.)

Packing

YOUR NEW MOTTO: "Small, light boxes." Just repeat it over and over to yourself. While packing, imagine that you'll have to carry every single box a quarter mile and then up four flights of stairs,

Worried you won't be able to find someone at your college to buy you beer? In 1997, 18 percent of college students were 35 years old or older, most of them as part time students. And 100 percent of them liked to have a good time!

Source: www.idahoea.org

which may well be the case if your school has parking issues or a mail center on the other side of campus. Even if everything you own would fit beautifully in one big-mama box, don't do it, because you'll be hating life on move-in day.

YOUR OTHER NEW MOTTO: There's a library at school so leave books at home. Books are heavy and difficult to move. For the books you deem pertinent, spread them out among different boxes, as opposed to three huge well-organized but unliftable boxes.

The Great Computer Decision

As email becomes the major means of communication between teachers and students, computers are becoming a necessity in higher education. (You won't know about the 24-hour extension your teacher offers at 11pm if you don't have e-mail.) For this reason, many schools now give students computers during freshman week and automatically add the fee into tuition. If your school doesn't do this, you can often buy a used computer quite cheaply, or a new computer through your school's computer office. Keep in mind that your computer will be used heavily and will probably be outdated by the time you graduate, so this may not be the time to purchase the most expensive computer ever. If you feel you can't afford a computer, contact your financial aid office—many schools have hidden clauses that will actually fund your computer.

Before you buy, ask yourself what your primary computer use will be. As a humanities major, all you'll really need is Internet access and a word-processing program. If you're considering a multimedia-oriented major, such as computer science or design, you may need to run complicated programs, so make sure your computer is appropriately powerful. Either way, check to see that your computer has an operating system and Internet access compatible with your school's network.

"My advice to incoming freshmen: put your name on everything from CDs to underwear. You'll thank me someday.

—Senior, Williams College

Laptop vs. Desktop

Laptops are a wonderful asset to college life. Not only are they easy to transport on move-in day, but you can write your papers wherever you'd like, study anywhere, and be portable in general. Laptops are also helpful on vacations, allowing you to easily take your schoolwork with you, particularly

if you're vacationing during the semester. How else would you send in your term paper from a hotel in West Palm Beach?

Desktops are fine as well, though not quite as convenient. Many students prefer desktops, and they seem to be doing OK. They have the advantage of being harder to steal and often come with faster processors for less money. The choice is yours.

Viruses and The Computer Lab

Colleges often have wonderful computer labs in various corners of campus that will suit you fine when your computer spontaneously dies. However, *beware* of viruses—most computer labs are the cyber equivalent of Typhoid Mary. Always virus scan disks before putting them back in your own computer. (This implies that you should have an anti-virus program on your computer.

Computers usually come with them, and many are available for free online.)

Bikes and Cars

During your visits to schools, make sure to find out whether most students use cars, bikes, or their own two feet. Most schools are populated with bicyclists, so a bike could never hurt. However, bikes have extremely high theft rates, particularly in urban schools, so it's advisable to buy a cheap bike—say under fifty dollars (used is fine). College is not the place to bring your $400 super nice bike, because while it may still be super nice in four months, it will no longer be yours. Rollerblades are often a good solution for schools with ample flat pavement.

If few students drive cars at your school, it's advisable to leave your ride at home, unless

Worried about "the Freshman 15," the 15 pounds college freshmen are said to gain as they adjust to new eating habits? A 2001 study at the University of Alabama at Tuscaloosa may put you at ease: the study found that of the 58 subjects studied, men tended to stay at around the same weight during their freshman year, while women gained an average of four pounds.

you don't mind being Chauffeur to the World. Everyone you know will want to borrow your car, and once you say yes to one person, you'll have to say yes to everyone. Also, check to see what the parking rates are. The more urban your college is, the more expensive parking will be. If you do bring your car, you'll be in charge of car maintenance, which often makes the car not worth the annoyance, not to mention the price. (What do you do when your car breaks down five miles from school and you have a midterm in four hours that you haven't crammed for yet?) Best advice: Leave the car at home initially, and if you decide you really want one, bring it after Christmas break.

The Budget

After the buying bonanza, you'll need a budget. Sometime before you leave for school, jot down your expected school income and expenses, just so you'll have an idea of how much can be spent each week in college. You'd be surprised how quickly money (and visible abdominal musculature) can disappear over midnight pizza breaks, not to mention laundry. Depending on your financial situation, it might be advisable to not work your freshman fall, or at least not for the first few weeks, so you can get into an academic schedule before you need to schedule work hours. Many students end up changing jobs halfway through freshman year anyway, finding a job that better fits their new lifestyle.

Glossary

ACT American College Testing, an exam that some colleges will accept in lieu of the SAT. Guessers do well on this one, because the ACT does not penalize for incorrect answers. It's popular in the South and Midwest. The test is subject-based, broken into four sections: reading, math, English, and science reasoning, so don't take it early, because you may not have covered the material yet.

admissions officer The person who decides whether or not you're going to their college, a.k.a., God. Keep in mind that despite his or her omniscient powers, this person is indeed human, and appreciates interesting, thought-provoking applications.

advanced placement exams (APs) Those wonderful "college level" exams that descend on you from the sky to create two hell weeks during your junior and senior springs. Doing well on these exams can get you out of equally hellish, semester-long college introductory courses. Sponsored by the College Entrance Examination Board.

athletic recruitment The process by which high school athletes get admitted to schools they otherwise would not get into, often with scholarship money. The pairing of athletics and strong academics is always a winning combination in the admissions office.

binding A legal obligation to attend a school once accepted. When you apply to a school with a binding admissions policy, if they accept you, you're going there.

For more information about financial terms, see the terms section in our chapter on financial aid.

burn-out The process by which you begin to hate everything related to academics, extracurricular activities, and life in general, usually the result of nonsensical perfectionism. A common malady among those who try to "do everything" through high school and into college.

certificate programs College-level programs that provide job skill certification in any number of fields, such as computer programming. Certificates can serve as a stepping stone to eventual college admission, or provide college students with a large enough salary to pay their way through college. College graduates will sometimes enter certificate programs to pick up additional job skills.

CLEP Exams sponsored by the college board that cover first- and second-year college course material. We're not quite sure which colleges accept these scores for credit, but apparently some do, so check it out.

clothes The attire with which you costume yourself each day, in avoidance of both frostbite and charges of indecent exposure. Once in college, you'll find yourself buying more clothes, particularly underwear, to reduce the frequency with which you have to do laundry.

College Board The supposedly non-profit association that runs the SAT I & II, PSAT, CLEP, and AP exams. They also run a number of programs that no one has ever heard of, meant to connect students to college opportunities.

college counselor The (easy now; these people make up a good portion of your readership) helpful faculty member of your high school who is employed to help students gain admission to quality universities. If your school's college counselor is lacking, private college counselors exist in abundance.

college mail The unbelievably large quantities of packages, parcels, and junk mail you will receive from colleges in the latter years of high school. Your name is placed on their mailing lists via the college entrance exams you take through the College Board.

Common Application The most exciting invention since sliced bread. (It predates email.) Common applications ask general information and broad-based essay questions that are accepted by most schools, saving you time. Still, many pretentious schools, such as Princeton University, require you to fill out their own personal applications, and answer vague questions like "If you were an admissions officer at Princeton, how would you evaluate candidates for admissions?" (Your answer: "I would accept the snobbiest students possible.") Harvard University accepts the common application.

community college Smaller, local colleges that often offer two-year degrees. Community college can serve as a stepping stone between high school and admission to a four-year degree program. Many advanced students take classes at their local community college during high school, allowing them to count for high school course credit.

community service Helping others in your community in a constructive manner, usually without pay. Admissions officers love to see this in your application, anything from picking up trash along the highway to working with hospice patients in your free time.

cyber applications Now that we're in the Age of Technology, you don't need to buy stamps to apply for college. Lots of schools have online applications on their websites, so sending in applications is a click away. If you do use cyberapps, call a few days later to make sure your application was received.

culture shock The affliction of being totally overwhelmed by your new college. Culture shock is most common among international students, who have to adjust to the double whammy of a new college *and* a new country. It usually passes within a month or so.

deferment A college's way of saying, "We don't want you right now, but we might still want you later, but we're not sure, so we're going to make you wait for our decision for four agonizing months." Academically qualified students who aren't accepted in early admissions will often find themselves deferred to regular admissions.

diversity Student variety. Though this term is most commonly used in reference to ethnic background, colleges seek out a wide range of talents and upbringing in their student populations.

Early Action A wonderful program by which students can apply to a college early without a binding contract—i.e., if accepted, the student is not obligated to attend. Though early action highly reduces the stress on high schoolers who don't know where they want to spend the next four years of their lives, few schools use it. Most colleges opt for early decision instead.

Early Decision The early application program of most elite colleges, whereby students apply to their first-choice colleges by November 1 or November 15 of their senior fall. If accepted, the decision is binding, and the student must attend that college. Can be highly stressful.

Early Decision II A few schools, such as Middlebury College, offer two rounds of early decision applications. Applications are due in early January, and students learn their fate well before regular decision applicants hear back.

excellence The term you want admissions officers to use to describe your endeavors. Brilliance in motion.

FAFSA Federal Application For Student Aid. Once filled out, it's worth thousands and thousands of dollars. If you're lucky, your parents will fill it out for you.

fat envelope A well-girthed envelope that will come in the mail from your first-choice college, proclaiming your admission to their school. It's fat because there are lots of forms to fill out. However, keep in mind that many early decision acceptance letters are only a page because the forms for the coming year aren't ready until the spring.

financial aid Monetary aid given to you by your college so that you can afford to go there. Financial aid reflects financial need, and under federal law, is not allowed to reflect other talents (i.e. a school that doesn't give athletic scholarships is not allowed to give an amazing gymnast an extra ten thousand dollars of federal aid.) Financial aid comes in the form grants and loans.

extracurricular activities The main consideration of college admissions officers after academic performance. Do one or two in high school, and be good at them.

flu shots Your only way of preventing a debilitating mid-November illness both during your senior fall and your freshman fall. They're often free, so get one.

good roommate A sensitive, caring, friendly person who in no way imposes their strange habits on your life and doesn't mind proofing your papers and spontaneous 1 A.M. dance contests.

grade grubbing The act of placing your lips...

Greek life Social organizations characterized by confusing Greek symbols and beer. The social lives of many campuses surround fraternities and sororities, which subsequently pop up in the media with great frequency after being banned from various campuses.

gut courses Ridiculously easy college classes that leave you with ample time to experience your campus's social life. You can always spot a gut course by its slang title around campus, such as "Rocks for Jocks" or "Science for Retards."

Harvard University The superb institution attended by the authors of this book. In fact, the author of this glossary is currently neglecting her ample Harvard homework to write this glossary.

hell roommate The extremely strange person with an addiction to plucking who will be assigned to share a closet-sized space with you for your entire freshman year

homeroom That boring place you go each morning before classes start, led by a teacher to whom you should give inordinate amounts of attention with an eventual glowing letter of recommendation in mind. Kiss it goodbye after high school.

I-20 Form The form international students need to apply for an American student visa. If you plan on seeing anything of America other than her airports and embassies, fill it out.

international applicant Applicants to American colleges who live abroad. Some students have been known to use foreign addresses to fall under this category, but we're not sure why.

interview attire Think maximum skin coverage, minimal piercings. Conservative.

International Baccalaureate (IB) A two-year sequence of courses, designed to fulfill international academic standards, culminating in six or seven exams that can count for college course credit. Though IBs used to be the international equivalent of AP exams, they're cropping up in high schools all over the country.

Ivy League The crème de la crème of American universities, including Brown, Columbia, Cornell, Dartmouth, Harvard, Pennsylvania (University of), Princeton, and Yale. Not at all ironically, most of them really do have ivy growing up the walls of their academic buildings.

leadership 1) A large, leading boat—just kidding. 2) Admissions officers eat this stuff up. Your student leading activities show your maturity, organizational ability, and social skills.

legacy To have had a family member previously attend your college. Being a legacy is helpful in the admissions process, particularly for early decision schools. Colleges know they are almost guaranteed alumni donations from entire families that have attended their school, though it is not an automatic admissions ticket. Having your father donate a library is always an automatic admissions ticket though, whether or not he attended the school.

letters of recommendation The letters your high school teachers will write on your behalf to colleges, and the only objective view of your character and ability that admissions offices will see. Make sure that the teachers who write your recommendations really do like you and can testify to your intelligence.

major Your projected field of study in college. If an application asks and you're not sure, put "undecided." Though advice abounds about putting down rare majors to make yourself more "different," the percentage of students who change their minds once they reach college is well over 50 percent. So put down what you think you're going to study, and expect that you won't study it.

meal plan Your major source of nourishment once at college, along with Diet Coke and beer. We highly recommend signing up for it, at least for the first semester.

Meningitis vaccine Meningitis most commonly afflicts college freshmen. Get vaccinated.

minority applicants Not white and Anglo-Saxon. You're at an advantage in the admissions office, unless you're Jewish or Asian, in which case you're on equal footing with everyone else.

National Merit honors Those who score in the top 5 percent of the nation on their junior fall PSAT. Students who score in the top 1 percent are deemed National Merit Finalists, and are eligible for National Merit Scholarships, which have much more to do with what companies your parents work for than with your academic ability.

NCAA National Collegiate Athletic Association. The NCAA is the umbrella for collegiate athletics. They enforce lots of student-athlete rules that are meant to encourage academics and fair play, but frequently end up being a major inconvenience.

NCAA eligibility Guidelines you must follow to be qualified for athletic recruitment. Basically, you have to not fail high school and fill out some forms.

need-blind Admissions offices that don't consider student financial need when going through applications. Only schools with large endowments, and therefore good financial aid programs, can afford to do this. Technically, the financial need form should be separate from a student's application. However, much can be deduced about a student's financial situation from an address and school, and admissions officers know which students have waived the application-fee out of financial need.

non-binding Applying to schools without an obligation to attend if accepted. Regular applications are almost all non-binding; early decision applications are usually binding.

parental paranoia Parental obsession with the college choosing and application process. Parental paranoia can manifest itself in many forms, including parents who want to visit *every* school with you, parents who hound you to fill out college applications six months in advance, and parents who really want you to get into an elite college, but never want their baby to leave home. Your only option is to cope, and know you'll be moving out in a few short months.

Pell Grants The largest and most common college federal aid program. Pell Grants usually make up the bottom of a financial aid package, on top of which other grants and scholarships are added.

PLUS loans College loans from the government or that are not based on financial need. After undergoing a credit check, any family can qualify.

prefrosh The designation as "almost-a-freshman." You've been accepted to college, but you're not quite there yet. A virtually responsibility-free place to be, so enjoy it.

prefrosh weekend Fun. Many schools offer their pre-freshmen an opportunity to descend onto campus for a weekend, offering a wide realm of wholesome activities. The nighttime activities you will witness are not so wholesome. Please keep in mind that alcohol can cause severe intoxication.

private schools Colleges that provide the majority of their own funding, as opposed to colleges that are slaves to the Federal or State Government.

prospective college list The list of colleges that you'd like to learn more about. The list should come into existence no later than early in your junior year.

public schools Colleges that receive the majority of their funding from state and federal government. These colleges often have high quotas for in-state students.

PSAT Preliminary Scholastic Aptitude Test. A test that many students take during the sophomore year and junior year of high school as an indicator of future SAT performance. Students who do well on the PSAT can earn recognition from the National Merit Association.

reach school That school that you put on your prospective college list in a moment of optimism. You know you're probably not going to get in, but what the hell, why not try it?

recruited athlete A high schooler in whom college coaches show active interest, and try to lure to their school through constant phone calls and promises of scholarship money.

regular admissions The not-early time to apply. Deadlines are usually around January 1st.

rejection Denial of a request to go on a date by the one person you had your heart set on dating, making you positive that your life is over.

reply card The postcard saying you're going to attend the school you were just accepted to. If you don't return the card, you're not going to the school.

rolling admissions A rare but wonderful policy in which admissions officers review applications as they arrive from October through January and send acceptance letters right away. Fantabulous.

ROTC Reserve Officers Training Corps. Better known as America's biggest scholarship program. If you don't mind waking up at 6 A.M. to do push-ups, wearing fatigues to class once a week, and serving your country for a few years after college, the military will give you lots of college scholarship money.

Scholarship 1) A boat for academics—kidding again. 2) Financial money toward college based on merit, usually either athletic or academic. Division I schools are happy to fund entire educations for students who can run fast.

safety school Yale University, go to www.safetyschool.org

SAT I Scholastic Aptitude Test. The multiple-choice mental capacity test that partially decides your college destination, though many schools are moving toward emphasizing other aspects of the application.

A bit of SAT trivia—the following question is from the first SAT in 1926: Count each N in this series that is followed by a P next to an O if the O is not followed by a T. Tell how many N's you count.

NONTQMNOTMONOONQMNNOQNOTONAMONOM

(Don't worry, it's gotten much harder.)

SAT II An hour-long subject-based test, known to your older siblings as the Achievement Tests. Most colleges require that you take the Writing SAT II, a math SAT II, and one other of your choice. Many students take a foreign-language exam to count for college credit.

SAT III We just made this one up to confuse you

seven sisters The female college response to the Ivy League. The schools include Holyoke, Smith, Radcliffe (which no longer exists), Barnard, Wellesley, and are better known as the "ritzy girls schools."

special needs Students who need additional support to adequately function, either physically or academically. Colleges are required by law to be accommodating to all special needs students.

spinning yourself Making yourself look like Grade-A college material on paper, as this book explains.

Stafford Loans Government loans for students who are attending college part-time, regardless of financial need.

staying calm The practice of not freaking out during the college admissions process. Parents are very poor at this lifestyle technique.

study abroad Taking high school or college classes in foreign countries. College admissions officers look kindly on high school study abroad programs as a sign of maturity. College study abroad is just plain fun.

summer The warmest three months of the year, where you have a chance to do whatever you want and show colleges how cool you are. We recommend joining the circus.

supplementary material Additional information that you want colleges to see, most commonly artistic work. Whatever you do, make sure it's good.

suppressed scores Test scores that are not shown to colleges. For some tests, such as the SAT II, you choose which exams admissions officers see. For other tests, such as the SAT I, admissions officers see every score you've ever received. In other words, if you're hungover, wait until the next administration of the test.

sympathy grades High grades received solely due to the amount of guilt a teacher feels in giving you the grades you really deserve. Sympathy grades and earned grades are indistinguishable on an academic transcript.

thank you notes The pleasant notes of gratitude and appreciation you send to every person you meet who is associated with your college of choice, filled with open mentionings of your desire to attend their school.

TOEFL Test of English as a Foreign Language. Most international students are required to take this as proof of their fluency in English. If you've spoken English since childhood, feel free to contact your college and explain (in English) that this would be a waste of time for you.

transfer student A student who dislikes their college after a semester or two (or three), and applies to a new college. Arriving on a new campus after freshman year can be rough, so transfer students tend to bond with each other.

tuition The money you pay your school for academics (as opposed to room and board). In the Ivy Leagues, classes break down to around $100 per class hour.

virtual tours The opportunity for you to experience a campus through your computer screen. Though often cornily wholesome, virtual tours can save you a long trip to visit a place you'll hate on sight.

waitlist The List from Hell, where your college career is decided by another confused high schooler's decision to accept or decline admission to your number-one school. Confused high schoolers reliably take their sweet time making decisions.

weather The explanation behind the torrential arctic winds pummeling your new northern campus that was so pristine and rosy in August.

work-study common part of financial aid packages, allowing students to get jobs for which the government will pay 70 percent of their wages. Work-Study is great, because since you only cost $3 an hour, everyone wants to hire you. Library jobs are particularly easy.

U.S. News and World Report rankings The most looked-at college rankings in America, which rank everything from best overall colleges to most diverse campuses to highest graduation rates. Their methods of weighing various aspects of college life are always under fire in the media, particularly by colleges that didn't do so well.

About the Authors

Danielle Charbonneau, Editor

Danielle Charbonneau is a junior English concentrator at Harvard University. Born in Boston and raised by her amazingly cool family on Cape Cod, Dani's goals in life are to be a writer with a cult following and to one day eat lunch with Tom Robbins. Dani owes her love of words to a fantastic bunch of English teachers in high school, and a family that persistently demanded poetry from her through childhood. She has spent her time at college writing for the on-campus humor magazine *Satire V,* and working fun jobs in Cambridge, such as "lackey" for NPR's nationally broadcast "Car-Talk." To all the kids being picked on in high school Dani has this message: work hard and remember, getting in is the best revenge.

Arianne Cohen, Associate Editor

Arianne Cohen is a junior at Harvard College. In high school she declared that she would never attend one of those "snobby" Ivy League schools; instead, she was going to go to the University of California at Berkeley, where she would be "cool" for four years. After five college recruiting trips and three casual visits, she changed her mind and went to Cambridge, where she spent her first two years on the varsity swimming and water polo teams. She has since dried off to devote her time to campus publications, yoga, running, and the fine art of "hanging out."

Writers

MIKE YANK. Mike Yank, a senior at Harvard, hails from Charlottesville, Virginia, the home of UVA, Monticello, and the Dave Matthews Band. Mike is a history of science major concentrating on the sociology of paranormal phenomena, and is writing a thesis on journals that publish studies about ESP and UFOs. A member of the Harvard Lampoon, the world's oldest continuously published humor magazine, he loves writing comedy and plans to move to the big city after he graduates and to beg for a job writing for a sit-com. He also enjoys singing in and arranging songs for the Harvard Lowkeys, a fifteen-person co-ed a cappella group. If you are looking for some cool bands to get into before you head off to college, Mike recommends Neutral Milk Hotel, Built to Spill, the Apples in Stereo, Beulah, Elf Power, Ladybug Transistor, and, of course, Radiohead.

TOM MILLER. A junior English major at Harvard, Tom graduated from Wauwatosa West High School in Wauwatosa, Wisconsin in 1999. A tuba player, runner, swimmer, and thespian, he was dead set on attending Caltech and studying astronomy. After changing his mind literally twenty-four hours before the reply deadline, he decided Boston was more his style and became the first kid from Tosa West to attend Harvard in twenty years. An aspiring writer/doctor/astronaut, Miller spends his spare time composing boring short stories, acting with On Thin Ice (an occasionally funny improv comedy team) and running marathons.

KATHY LEE. From Danville, California, Kathy is a junior majoring in government, which is fancy-talk for political science. Her passions include painting, writing, and frittering away her youth. When in California, she lives with her parents, two of the coolest cats to ever prowl the wild streets of Danville, and her brother, who amazes her with his charm, intelligence, and inability to grow a mustache. She has no idea what she wants to do with her degree, but hopes that one day she can realize her dream of becoming the world's greatest caber tosser. She is seriously muscular. If she were a dinosaur, she would be Buffasaurus Rex. Above all, she tries to savor every moment of life, recalling the wise words of one of the Marx brothers: "Time flies like an arrow; fruit flies like a banana." Word.

OLIVIA COWLEY. Olivia is currently a senior at Harvard University. Originally from New York City, she now lives in Newport, Rhode Island. An avid traveler, she has spent several summers working for Let's Go Publications, as a Researcher-Writer in South America and Southeast Asia, as the Editor of *Let's Go Spain & Portugal*, and as a Managing Editor. She sympathizes with all the users of this book, as she too is beginning the application process again—this time to law school. Olivia would like to thank Daniel Parish and the College Counseling Office at Phillips Exeter Academy; the Story Street boys, Matthew Adler, Meg Austin, Dimple Chaudhary, Kelsey Doub, Emily Griffin, Dina Hasiotis, Ashley Kircher, Rommy Martinez and Rob, Didi, and Savannah Cowley.

With Special thanks to Denise Cinquegrana, '02, for all her knowledge of the transfer application process . . . and Melissa Rudolph, '01, for her mad sick designs.

The staff would also like to thank Brad Olson, '03, for his unending support and cute, smiling face.

let's go
travel guides

www.letsgo.com

written by students for students